A Little Book of
Altar Magic

D. J. Conway

THE CROSSING PRESS
FREEDOM, CALIFORNIA

Copyright © 2000 by D. J. Conway
Cover design by Chitose Baba
Cover photo by Nicole Lasher
Interior design by Karen Narita
Printed in the USA

For information on bulk purchases or group discounts for this and other Crossing Press titles, please contact our Special Sales Manager at 800/777-1048.

www.crossingpress.com

Library of Congress Cataloging-in-Publication Data on file
ISBN: 1-58091-052-1

Contents

Chapter 1—The History of Altars   1

Chapter 2—How to Erect and Prepare an Altar   9

Chapter 3—Symbols and Sacred Objects   16

   Sacred Animals   18

   Ritual Objects   29

   Colors and Elements   51

   Stones   59

   Trees   63

   Herbs   71

   Oils   77

   Flowers   80

   Deities   91

   Angels and Archangels   111

   Saints   113

Chapter 4—Building Special Altars   121

   Love   123

   Prosperity   124

   Protection   125

   Thanksgiving   126

   Spiritual Growth   127

   Finding a Job   128

Making a Decision   130
Recovering from Divorce   131
Healing   133
In Memory of Lost Loved Ones   134
Dedication to God/Goddess/Saint   136

Resources   137

Bibliography   141

CHAPTER 1

The History of Altars

Altars have been used from almost the beginning of human civilization, as far back as the Paleolithic Age. Yet many people today do not understand exactly what an altar is outside of a religious structure, and do not believe they can set up personal altars in their homes. Nevertheless, on a subconscious level, we set up varieties of altars without giving any conscious thought to the process.

It is common to see groupings of family photos arranged on shelves, tables, or pianos. Many people place clusters of sentimental objects or collections of various kinds in glass-front cabinets or on shelves in various rooms of their homes. It is not uncommon to see displays of collections of beer cans, thimbles, dragons, model cars, or similar objects. These are all done without conscious thought or planning, except that we "want to." But why do we feel drawn to do this?

Carl G. Jung named the deepest part of our subconscious

mind "the collective unconscious," and said that it connects every person to every single ancestor and provides access to everything that has been known in the past. It seems that the collective unconsciousness within each of us is persuading us to build a personal altar, just as our ancestors did. The problem is, we seldom stop our busy minds long enough to listen to the collective unconscious and learn from it.

The wall of beer cans is a type of informal altar to the gods Dionysus or Bacchus, both deities of the vine, wine, and good times. Model cars may well be a subconscious tribute to the fleet-footed Mercury or to Helios and his sun chariot. Thimbles are symbols of weaving goddesses such as Spider Woman, Ixchel, the Fates, and Athena. Collections of dragons, wizards, and the like are subconscious attempts to tap ancient magic and mystical knowledge. Groupings of family photos can be remembrances of the dead in the hope they will aid us, or sympathetic magic to link the dead with the living. A collection of frog figures may be a subconscious plea to ancient fertility goddesses.

This penchant for informal altars cuts across social and cultural lines. In fact, preparing an altar is a multicultural experience. Unknowingly, humans are constantly building altars around them. Perhaps we should give more thought to the process, thus learning how to enhance our daily lives and spiritual growth.

Archaeologists have discovered the very earliest permanent sacred altars to be deep inside caves, with narrow, treacherous paths leading to them. Their difficult access made the journey a determined, conscious effort. The caves were highly spiritual places, not to be entered lightly, for they symbolized the eternal, everflowing womb of the Goddess and the cauldron of primordial energy. Within them, people used magic for hunting and performed rites of passage including initiation. People and their tribal shamans visited these secret caves whenever their clan migrations brought them back to that area.

However, it is likely that the migrating people of the Paleolithic cultures also carried small Goddess images with them as they traveled from one area to another in search of wild game and other food. These people would create a temporary altar at the hearth they made inside each cave or rocky shelter they entered. The strange little rotund female figures they used to represent the Goddess were shaped with exaggerated belly, breasts, and buttocks to symbolize the Great Mother who gave birth to everything in the world. The faces of these figurines were only vaguely formed. Some figurines had their legs tapered to a point that could be stuck into the ground; others had flat, widespread bottoms, so they could be placed on any fairly level surface. All were quite small, just the size for carrying easily from one place to another.

Later statues became slightly more sophisticated, but most still retained only the suggestion of facial features, like their earlier counterparts. Where the Goddess of Willendorf and those of Grimaldi, Lespugue, and Sireuil are very stylized and exaggerated in body form, the Minoan snake goddesses appear more human in proportion. In addition to being decorated with spirals or meanders (wavy lines), the Minoan figures now hold two recognizable snakes. This evolution of form continues until we find the beautiful, very human, statues of Egypt, China, the Middle East, Greece, and Rome.

The earliest caves were decorated with vivid, life-like paintings of animals, handprints, and other symbols, all representing abstract spiritual and magical ideas concerned with sustaining life and bringing comfort in death. Later, when villages were established and the clans no longer roamed from place to place, human-built shrines became more elaborate. Although the shrine itself is a symbolic cave, the floors of some in the Minoan culture are carefully paved with seashells and roughly carved, colorful stones, with the walls painted just as vividly as those found in the mystical, secret caves. The symbolism's representation becomes more direct.

From the incised decorations on the surviving deity figures, the fabulous paintings on cave walls, and the remains of later shrines, archaeologists have learned that certain symbols held great meaning for our ancestors. Meanders represent water and the sacred snake of life. Lozenges stand for fertility, while the triangle means the feminine and regeneration, just as the cave itself did. The crescent represents the lunar cycle and energy. A cupmark cut into a stone held water, symbolizing the sacred water that flowed from the Goddess of life. Footprints painted on cave walls refer to the healing force and guidance of the Goddess, while hands are symbols of Her divine powers against evil. Eyes, spirals, and coiled snakes represent the cosmic life force that is an endless source of energy. An X symbolizes death and regeneration, and is similar to both the butterfly and the hourglass.

Archaeologists have found evidence of two types of shrine through every age: the permanent and the mobile. Two things become clear from the study of the religious practices of ancient cultures. The first type was originally a natural site, such as a special cave, grove of trees, hilltop, or power spot. What we would call the altar was usually a naturally formed rock that happened to be within the sacred place. Except for engravings on rocks or paintings on cave walls, the sacred place was not transformed in any way.

The second type of shrine indicates that these early people understood that any place could be made sacred by erecting a temporary altar. This simple portable altar, consisting of a

Goddess statue, was of great value since Paleolithic clans seldom stayed in one place for very long. They needed a place to worship and to perform their sympathetic magic while they followed the migrating herds of wild game.

These two types of shrine persist even after people began to settle permanently in villages. It seems that although people gathered together in one place for special ceremonies, they liked the idea of having their own personal altars at home.

The elements of Earth, Water, and Fire were very important to the early migrating peoples. Their lives depended upon fire for protection, warmth, and light; they considered that the earth provided their source of food; and they knew their existence depended upon a ready source of water. Much later, our ancestors added the element of Air to the list when they realized that this invisible substance was needed for breathing and that wind brought storms and rain. Spirit, the traditional fifth element, had always been important, for the elusive power of Spirit tied the living to the dead and held the promise of rebirth.

Today, we find the same symbolism in our modern places of worship. Some religions have a definite altar, while in others the altar has become only a raised platform for the minister and choir. Non-Christian religions often have special cabinets for their holy books. Sacred spaces are decorated with flowers, candles, and often pictures or statues of deities, saints, or gurus. Sometimes, holy water is kept by the door, and grape juice or wine is offered to the participants. Singing or chanting and prayer are usually part of the service.

But what do we do at home, in our private places? Statues of saints are common in Catholic households. A cross is a familiar symbol in other Christian homes. Non-Christian homes have statues or symbols of their deities, often surrounded by flowers, candles, and other symbolic offerings. These are consciously made altars, places we make sacred for our spiritual growth and comfort.

Those who do not attend any organized church or temple or do not profess any belief in any deities are still influenced by the collective unconscious mind to build altars. Subconsciously, they are drawn to build little informal altars of collections of items that appeal to them. With some thought and attention, these altars can add positive energy to our lives.

We need to realize that conscious intent in building an altar can create a positive, spiritual atmosphere that will improve our everyday lives. Altar building crosses all cultural lines and is not necessarily connected to any religion. Taking this action merely says that you wish to connect with the unlimited pool of cosmic energy that sustains the entire universe. This connection may be made to manifest certain desires in your life or simply to say "thank you" to a higher power for what you already have. An altar can be permanent, changeable, or temporary, according to your needs. The bottom line is that you should be building your altars with conscious intent and understanding of what you are doing.

Intentionally building an altar helps you to step outside yourself and whatever everyday troubles you may have. Using an altar helps you to elevate yourself in order to see your surroundings and conditions more clearly. It helps you to clarify what you want and why you want it. Although you may choose objects for your altar subconsciously, not completely understanding why you made the choice, the very act of creating an altar teaches you to listen to your subconscious mind and its messages. You become more centered and at peace with yourself. When you are centered, positive energy and happiness flow into your life. Isn't that what we all truly desire?

CHAPTER 2

How to Erect and Prepare an Altar

Joseph Campbell said that sacred space is a place where wonder can be glimpsed. Building an altar (or altars) in your home can fill your life with wonder, for the presence of an altar makes any place sacred. Creating an altar opens you to the spiritual dimension, whatever path you choose to take. It allows you to express your personal glimpse of the divine in whatever way you imagine it. It helps you to integrate the sacred into your personal life, for altars are places of centering and rebalancing. It draws on subconscious thoughts, making you receptive to the sacred in life.

Building an altar requires four stages of preparation: thinking out and clarifying your reasons for doing so, planning the project, acknowledging the emotions behind this decision, and actually building the altar. These steps are no different from what we should be doing when we make every major decision in our lives. The whole experience is a process of discovering more about yourself, how you perceive things, and what symbols and objects mean to you.

What do you need to create an altar and make a sacred place? Really, not much. There is no need to run out and spend lots of money. Begin with what you have on hand. Most people are pack rats of a sort and tend to accumulate items they like. Look closely at your possessions. You will be surprised at what you find.

The first thing you will need is something on which to arrange the symbols and objects you choose for your altar. An altar space can be anything: a small shelf, a table, a covered box set in a corner, the top of a dresser, or one corner of the coffee table. The important thing is simply a flat surface, which does not need to be large or elaborate.

If you wish your altar to be private, arrange it in a place not readily visible to everyone, perhaps in your bedroom. If you wish to energize certain rooms of your home and do not care about your altars being seen, you can place them wherever you wish.

It is not unusual to find tiny altars in kitchens today. These may contain shiny copper molds, pictures of the family and pets, or perhaps a small statue of the Virgin Mary or the goddess Kuan Yin. At one time, the hearth and cooking area was the most important part of every house, for it was here that the precious fire was kept burning and the food for survival cooked. And it was here that one could find a small statue of the Goddess and perhaps a kitchen deity. The symbolism is the same as eight thousand years ago, when people placed Goddess statues in the grain bins so that the food supply would never run out and so that occupants of the house would prosper.

According to the Chinese art of placement, called *feng shui*, situating an altar so that it faces the main door will permit the *chi*, or energy, to freely enter the house. This may go back to the centuries-old thought that the threshold of a house should be protected, and that sacred objects set near the entrance build a demarcation between the outer public world and the inner private one.

Feng shui is thousands of years old and still used, with remarkable results. The energy forces said to be promoted by this art are believed to determine or change the outcome of health, prosperity, and luck. If you wish to place your altars according to *feng shui*, consider these suggestions. The Chinese say that rectangular and square shapes are *yang*, or masculine, in nature and spin off energy, while circular shapes are *yin*, or feminine, and hold energy in balance. Both *yin* and *yang* objects should be used in the art of placement; wind chimes, mobiles, or small fountains will increase energy within the home.

The Chinese also carefully consider directions when placing altars. The south is connected with professional success, fortune, and fame, with the color red and images of birds also useful there. The west is for creativity, joy, and children; the color white and an image of a tiger will increase energy in these aspects. East is associated with health and growth; use green and a dragon here. The north is connected with money, career, and business, as well as the color black.

For information on the use of colors, the elements, objects, symbols, and the directions, see Chapter 3, which goes into detail on their historical uses and meanings.

Now that you have decided what you will use for your altar and where you will set it, you need to consciously choose what you will place on it. You may wish to have all goddess statues, or you may choose to have both god and goddess images. Perhaps you will have saints instead, or no images at all. Every altar will reflect the personality and spirituality of the person who erects it.

Using the four elements on an altar will bring the energies associated with these elements to your sacred space. Fire can be a candle; Air, incense; Earth, a stone or flowers; Water, a fountain or water in a vase. Or each of these elements might be portrayed in a picture that speaks to you. By placing the elements on your altar, you are subconsciously asking that balance come to your space and life.

Certain flowers and the wood of trees have traditional meanings and can be used to symbolize specific energies. So can objects, such as a pyramid, box, animal figurine, or stone. Or you may decide to incorporate images and objects that remind you of a person you wish to remember or an event or action you desire to accomplish. Listen with your heart, and choose what feels right to you.

If you burn candles on your altar, be certain that the candle is firmly set in a metal holder and is well away from anything flammable. The last thing you want is a devastating fire ruining your home. Incense is also a potential problem if not handled with care. Stick incense should be placed in a can of sand or a holder large enough not to tip over. Cone incense should be placed in an unbreakable, heat-resistant holder or on a bed of sand. If you burn paper requests at your altar, use a metal bowl or cauldron.

Chapter 4 gives several examples of altars erected for a specific purpose and the objects placed on them. These altars are eclectic and not especially based on any religion or lack thereof. Feel free to change them to incorporate your own ideas and desires.

It is a good idea to cleanse your altar periodically. Dust does accumulate, as does pet hair. Some people feel the need to cleanse their altar weekly by smudging or burning incense and sprinkling holy water. Others only clean when their instincts say it is necessary, or after negative people have been in the house and have touched the altar.

Try to cleanse your altar separately from your ordinary housecleaning, so you can concentrate on the action and not shatter the vibrations built up around the altar. Remove any dead flowers, clean up incense ashes, and trim candle drips. Rearrange or replace any items you wish.

If children are visitors or permanent residents, they will probably rearrange things on the altar. Take this in stride and be patient. As long as the children are not destructive, arranging an altar can be an enthralling pastime for them.

Altars can be erected in celebration, commemoration, to mark life's turning points, or to heal grief. They are also valuable in helping you to focus energy on a specific part of your life that you would like to improve or change. Grief altars are helpful in working through emotional pain, whether that pain arises from the loss of a loved one to death, divorce, or some other end of a relationship. Event altars keep you focused on a goal, such as paying off a mortgage or saving money for a long-desired trip. Altars are reminders of where we need to focus our attention, and that the spiritual is intertwined with the mundane and is never separate from it.

It does not matter how you view the word "spiritual" in

relationship to altars. Spiritual simply means acknowledging that there is a Power or Force greater than you. You may call it Goddess, God, or the Big Bang. Building an altar is a way of consciously reminding yourself that a powerful force of energy runs through the universe that anyone can tap into with a little effort. Whether you do positive or negative things with that force is up to you. However, remember that the type of energy you give out is what you get back, so it is safer and more productive to do only positive things.

Perhaps one of the most important things to remember about building an altar is that it should be done with joy, anticipation, and a sense of wonder. By your actions you are drawing spiritual energy into your everyday life. This cannot help but make changes for the better.

So build your altar as it pleases you, and be prepared for your life to open and expand in a way you never thought possible.

CHAPTER 3

Symbols and Sacred Objects

Through the centuries, humans have used many different symbols and objects as part of their individual and collective spiritual worship. Since the collective unconscious mind of every human, as described by Carl Jung, is connected to the symbols used by our ancestors through genetic memory, these objects and symbols still have deep meaning for us.

The subconscious mind does not speak in words, but only in nonverbal symbols. By using symbolic objects on your altars, you are communicating with your subconscious mind, the conduit through which flow psychic messages, spiritual communications, and extrasensory perception, all the little nudges and gut feelings that help us deal with life's difficulties. To open the door to the collective unconscious, one must enter through the subconscious mind. Until you establish a dialogue using symbols, the subconscious mind will not allow you to reach that deeper source of information.

Today, many people are attracted to ancient deities from around the world. This attraction may be to the deities of their ancestors, or it may come from a past life to which they still have strong ties. Renewing a relationship with the powers represented by these old goddesses and gods by placing representations of them on altars may help these people improve their lives.

For those who have no attraction to ancient deities, I have provided lists of angels, archangels, and saints. Petitions to these spiritual beings have brought about success and guidance in many people's lives.

By using any of the following images and objects on your altars, you are strengthening the spiritual energies that collect about your sacred places. By intensifying the energies, you deepen your spiritual experiences and hasten the creation of your desires.

SACRED ANIMALS

All around the world, various creatures have always represented certain deities and/or magical qualities. Using statues, photos, or drawings of animals on your altar can help you to invoke a specific energy you wish to manifest in yourself or in your life. These animals can be actual creatures, or they can be what are known as fabulous beasts, such as the unicorn.

Following is a list of creatures, both physical and fabulous, whose magical–spiritual qualities have been known and used by many cultures. Sometimes called shamanic or totem animals, their astral (nonphysical) equivalents frequently appear in meditations, shamanic journeys, and dreams. They act as guides and portents of things to come.

Adder, snake—Wisdom, cunning, defense, psychic energy, creative power, pure divine energy, beginning and ending, and understanding.

Badger—Tenacity and unyielding courage.

Bat—Gaining direction in difficult circumstances; avoiding obstacles, barriers, and troublesome people. In China, the bat is a symbol of good fortune and happiness; in Europe, a companion creature of the goddess Hel.

Bear—Stamina, harmony, protecting the self and the family, dreams, intuition, transformation, and astral travel. The bear was sacred to the Greek goddesses Callisto and Artemis.

Bee—Responsibility, cooperation, prosperity, and planning for the future. In the Indo-Aryan and Greek Orphic teachings, bees were thought of as souls. They were called the Little Servants of the Goddess by early matriarchies. Bee was also the title of Aphrodite's high priestess on Mount Eryx. The Greek goddess Demeter was sometimes called "the mother bee."

Blackbird—This bird denotes joy.

Boar, sow, pig—Cunning, intelligence, revenge, defense, knowledge of past lives, magic, protection of family, cooperation, prosperity, and health, death, and rebirth. The sow, in particular, represents magic, the Underworld, and deep knowledge of the Crone aspect of the Goddess. The sow was sacred to Astarte, Cerridwen, Demeter, Freyja, and the Buddhist aspect of the Goddess called Marici.

Bull, cow—The bull is a symbol of strength, potency, alertness, protection of the family, and knowing when to be aggressive. The cow represents gentleness and balance, but also fierce mother love and the life-giving and sustaining power of creation. In the beginning of human religious symbology, the bull was a lunar symbol of the Great Mother, with the horns emblematic of the crescent moon. Later, the bull became a symbol of sun gods such as Attis and Mithra, both associated with Cybele. The cow was associated with the Egyptian goddesses Hathor and Neith, and the Norse goddess Audhumla.

Butterfly—Reincarnation, beauty, love, transformation, joy, and freedom. To the ancient Greeks, the butterfly represented the soul. In Ireland, Cornwall, Mexico, and Siberia, white butterflies are still believed to be the spirits of the dead.

Cat (domestic)—Independence, discrimination, stealth, resourcefulness, healing, love, self-assurance, seeking hidden information, seeing spirits, and receiving protection when faced with a confrontational situation. In ancient Egypt, the cat was considered to be a lunar creature and was sacred to Bast and Isis. In other cultures, it was sacred to Artemis, Diana, and Freyja.

Cheetah—Swiftness, speed, and developing self-esteem; making events happen quicker.

Cobra—To the ancient Egyptians, the cobra symbolized spiritual and divine wisdom and protection. The Hindus saw the cobra as a representation of the kundalini force that rose through the seven chakras of the astral body.

Cock—Self-confidence.

Coyote—Cunning, shapeshifting, stealth, opportunity, creativity, and new life.

Crane—From China to the Mediterranean, the crane represented justice, longevity, dignity, wisdom, discipline, vigilance, and reaching deeper mysteries and truths.

Crocodile—To ancient Egyptians, this creature represented mindless fury and evil. However, they also said the crocodile could provide knowledge.

Crow—Trickery, boldness, skill, cunning, alertness, prophecy, and shapeshifting. A companion of the Celtic goddess Morrigan, the crow symbolized the creative power and spiritual strength found through the Crone aspect of the Goddess. The raven is similar.

Deer, hind, doe—A messenger from the Otherworld, the appearance of the deer traditionally signaled a guide for adventures of mystical value. This creature also represented contact with spirit guides and the gods; abundance, dreams, intuition, and psychic powers.

Dog, hound—Devotion, companionship, loyalty, willingness to follow through, alertness, and discovering hidden knowledge and the truth. Sacred to Underworld goddesses, dogs also represent our own subconscious judgment. Myth says that the Celtic god Nodens, a healer, could shapeshift into a dog. The Norse god Odin rode on his Wild Hunt with a pack of hounds, carrying out the wishes of the goddess Hel.

Dolphin, porpoise—Intelligence, communication, friendships, eloquence, freedom, speed, prudence, change, balance, and harmony. Sacred to the Greek goddess Themis, this creature also symbolized active seedforms within the sea-womb of creation.

Dove, pigeon—Often the symbol of a spiritual messenger between worlds, in the past this bird also represented peace and love, a meaning it still holds today. It was sacred to Aphrodite, Astarte, and Venus.

Dragon—This fabulous creature is a universal symbolic figure found in most cultures around the world, and has several, sometimes contradictory, meanings. The dragon represents cunning, knowledge, riches, protection, the ability to rise above and conquer obstacles, and instruction in spiritual matters.

Dragonfly—Dreams, breaking down illusions, mystic messages of enlightenment, and seeing the truth in any situation.

Eagle—Wisdom, long life, taking advantage of opportunities, keen insight, strength, courage, seeing the overall pattern of life, connecting with powerful spiritual beings, and the ability to reach spiritual heights.

Eel—Avoiding trouble.

Elephant—A sacred creature to the Hindus, the elephant represents the power of the libido, removal of obstacles and barriers, confidence, patience, tackling a new situation, strength, wisdom, and eternity.

Falcon—Astral travel and healing.

Fish—To many Mediterranean and Asian cultures, fish in general symbolized sexuality and fertility. They also represent the subconscious mind and divination.

Fox—The Greek god Dionysus was said to shapeshift into a fox on occasion; his Lydian priestesses wore fox skins and were called Bassarids. The fox denotes intelligence, cunning, wisdom, remaining unobserved, and avoiding trouble.

Frog—Moving quickly, keeping a low profile, fertility, a new cycle of life, and initiation and transformation. The Egyptian frog goddess Hekat was connected with birth.

Goose—New beginnings, inspiration, happiness in general, happy marriage, children, creativeness, and spiritual guidance in one's destiny.

Griffin—Great magic, power, facing the inner self, spiritual enlightenment, and understanding the relationship between psychic energy and cosmic force.

Hare, rabbit—Transformation, receiving hidden teachings and intuitive messages, quick thinking, divination, fertility, swiftness, and avoiding traps or dangerous situations. Hares and rabbits were sacred to lunar goddesses.

Hawk—Keen insight into situations, being observant, omens and dreams, and recalling past lives. In Egypt, the hawk was thought to represent the soul. Sacred to the god Horus, the hawk symbolized the inner vehicle for transformation. The hawk was also an animal of Apollo.

Hedgehog—Self-defense.

Heron—Dignity, watching for opportunities, patience, and the generation of life.

Hippopotamus—Birth of new ideas, pregnancy, life, and strength. The Egyptian hippopotamus goddess Ta-Urt also represented righteous fury.

Horse—Associated in several cultures with death and the Underworld, the horse was frequently sacred to ocean deities. It was considered to be a vehicle for journeying to the Underworld, where one could contact spirits of the dead. It also symbolized freedom, friendships, stamina, faithfulness, and a journey.

Hummingbird—Love and happiness.

Ibis—A bird of the Egyptian god Thoth, the ibis was symbolic of magic, spells, writing, and recordkeeping.

Leopard, panther—Swiftness, cunning, strength, aggressiveness, and perseverance. These animals were sacred to the Greek god Dionysus.

Lion, lioness—The male lion represents relaxation, strengthening family ties, power, majesty, courage, energy, releasing tension and stress. The lioness symbolizes strong, protective mother love, the ability to care for one's self and family, and the strength to defeat aggressors. The lioness was sacred to such goddesses as Hathor, Sekhmet, and Cybele, while the lion belonged to such male deities as Apollo, Chrysocomes, the Arabic Shams-On, and Mithra.

Lizard—Escape from danger, dreams, mental creations, keeping a low profile, and asking for guidance in difficult situations.

Lynx—Intelligence and long journeys.

Magpie—Boldness.

Monkey—Ingenuity when dealing with problems.

Mouse—Being inconspicuous.

Octopus—Symbolizes the unfolding of the creative–destructive process.

Otter—Magic, friendship, joy of life, finding inner treasures or talents, gaining wisdom, and recovering from a crisis.

Owl—To the ancient Egyptians, the owl symbolized death, night, and cold. However, to the Greeks, it represented wisdom, the moon, lunar mysteries, and initiations. This bird also symbolizes alertness, wisdom, magic, keen insight into obscure events, unmasking deceivers, dreams, shapeshifting, clairvoyance, and a messenger of hidden secrets. The owl was sacred to such goddesses as the Eye Goddess of the Mediterranean, Athena, Lilith, Minerva, Blodeuwedd, Anath, and Mari.

Peacock—Dignity, self-confidence, watchfulness, and divine justice. It was sacred to the goddesses Hera and Sarasvati.

Pegasus—Poetic inspiration, astral travel, and changing evil into good. It was sacred to the Greek goddess Medusa and to the Muses.

Phoenix—Renewal, rebirth, and spiritual growth.

Quail—Good luck and victory.

Raccoon—Creativeness when faced with a new problem.

Ram, sheep—Keeping your balance in upsetting situations, fertility, and new beginnings.

Rat—Slyness and being able to move inconspicuously.

Raven—This bird has long been considered a messenger from the spirit world and a guide to oracles and teachers of magic. Sacred to such Celtic goddesses as Rhiannon and Morrigan, the raven represents great magic, divination, eloquence, spiritual wisdom, prophecy, a change in consciousness, intelligence, and communicating with the Otherworld.

Salmon—Great magic, journeys, endurance, and spiritual wisdom.

Scarab beetle—Vitality, new life, and learning about past lives.

Seagull—Taking advantage of opportunities.

Seal—Guidance when facing a separation or divorce; protection from gossip.

Snail—This creature, with its spiral-shaped shell, represents the action of the primordial spiral of energy upon matter.

Sphinx—Initiation and the end of a cycle.

Spider—Creativity, new life, beginning a new project, and becoming pregnant. As a weaver, the spider symbolizes the spiraling energy of primordial matter and the Divine Center in the web of illusion.

Squirrel—Harmony with life, patience, endurance, changing with the times, preparing for the future, and moving to a higher level of consciousness.

Stag—This horned creature represents the animal passions within each human.

Stork—Sacred to the goddess Juno, the stork represents a messenger of new ideas and birth.

Swan—Dream interpretation, mystical knowledge, developing intuitive abilities, dignity, and following instincts. Sacred to such goddesses as Aphrodite, Venus, Sarasvati, and the Norse Valkyries, the swan also symbolizes a messenger from the Goddess and the satisfaction of a desire.

Tiger—Power, energy; facing an unpleasant situation and doing something about it.

Turtle, tortoise—Keeping alert for danger; patience, perseverance, long life. In the Far East, the turtle symbolized the cosmos and seeds of unformed matter that would subsequently manifest.

Unicorn—Purity of spirit, a link between the physical and spiritual realms, fame, prosperity, strength of mind, and developing personal power.

Vulture—Cycle of death and rebirth, spiritual counsel, destruction followed by rebirth, and prophecy. Sacred to the Egyptian goddesses Nekhbet and Mut.

Whale—Music, long life, family, friends, developing psychic and telepathic abilities, initiation and rebirth, and embracing the opposites of existence.

Wolf—This animal represents cunning, intelligence, independence, avoiding trouble and escaping pursuers, the ability to pass by danger invisibly, outwitting those who wish you harm, strength to fight when necessary, wisdom, dreams, intuition, transformation, strong protection, strength, and spiritual guidance. To the Egyptians and Romans, the wolf represented valor; the wolf-god Wepwawet was a companion of Isis and Osiris. Among the Norse, it symbolized the destructive powers of chaos; Odin had two great wolves by his side at all times. The wolf was sacred to the Roman Lupa or Feronia and was a symbolic animal of the Vestal Virgins.

Wren—Divination, joy, and finding your niche in life.

RITUAL OBJECTS

Throughout human history, certain symbols and physical objects have been used in ritual and art to represent spiritual ideas. Many of these physical and artistic metaphors are still being used in modern religions and are powerful symbols for spiritual development. They often appear spontaneously in dreams and visions.

Any object becomes sacred when it is used consciously for the proper reasons on an altar. The following list suggests items you might wish to use. However, any object that has meaning for you is just as appropriate.

Ankh—A life symbol of a cross with a loop on top, the ankh was used by the ancient Egyptians to represent eternal life and resurrection. The crook or crozier, also known as the Shepherd's Cross, is a similar symbol. The Egyptian god Osiris, in his role as Shepherd of Souls, carried a crook, as did the Greek Hermes. Use it to represent divine guidance and spiritual seeking.

Arrows—This emblem signifies divine intervention of both healing and killing power. To the Balkan god Perun, the arrow denoted lightning, long a symbol of illumination. A symbol of the god Apollo, the arrow also represents supreme power and the sun's fertile rays. Mars, Tyr, and Mithra were also associated with the arrow. Use the arrow to symbolize the direct path you plan to take.

Basket—A sign of fertility, passion, and birth, a basket of ivy in ancient Greece symbolized the Bacchanalian mysteries of Dionysus. In ancient Egyptian hieroglyphs, it represented the wholeness of divinity. Ceremonies to the Egyptian goddess Isis and the Greek Artemis featured sacred baskets. Place a basket on your altar to symbolize gathering what you need in life.

Bowl—A symbol of the universal womb, the bowl represents both nurturing and giving. Use it to hold special stones or paper requests.

Box—With a lid, this is a female symbol connected with the subconscious mind and the unknown. A box without a lid represents life or gifts coming to you; it represents the universal womb. As with the basket and bowl, you can place in the box requests written on pieces of paper or jewelry that you wish to empower.

Breasts—Breasts symbolize the source of life power and life-giving fluids from the Great Mother. Some of the earliest sacred images were little models of two breasts with a stem that could be pushed into the ground, thus holding the image on an altar or personal hearth. Breasts represent everyday material needs being met.

Bridge—Traditionally, the bridge is a link between heaven and earth, or between the subconscious and conscious minds. Bifrost was the astral bridge that spanned the heavens between Asgard and Midgard in Norse myth, while for the Israelites the bridge symbolized the Covenant between God and His people. An image of a bridge can represent the bridging of differences, making a transition from one cycle of life to another, or moving to a higher plane of consciousness.

Bridle—This is a symbol of control over the physical body and the emotional things that would motivate a person to react without clear thinking.

Caduceus—Most people are familiar with the wand with two entwined serpents as the emblem of the Greek god Hermes and healing. However, this emblem existed long before the Greeks used it. The Sumerian goddess Inanna is shown holding the caduceus as she stands under the Tree of Life. The double-headed snake was one of the emblems of Ningishzide, a healer god who was one of Ishtar's lovers. The caduceus is also found on stone tablets in India, in paintings by Native Americans, and in Aztec art. To the Romans, it was a symbol of moral equilibrium, while to Buddhists it represents the axis of the world with the kundalini of the chakras entwined about it.

Candles—Lighted candles symbolize personal spiritual enlightenment. When choosing a color, check the list on Colors and Elements for the meaning.

Cauldron—Long a holy object, the cauldron represents the belly-vessel of rebirth and transformation. It was associated with many goddesses, one of whom was the Celtic Cerridwen. Use a small cauldron to symbolize the churning, primordial matter from which you can draw energy to manifest your desires.

Cave—A womb symbol of the Goddess, the cave represents that which is concealed, something incubating, or the entrance to the subconscious mind.

Chalice, cup—Similar to the cauldron, the chalice has several meanings. Its primary meaning is rebirth and illumination. However, a filled chalice represents the bounty of life coming to you from a higher power, while an empty chalice is the receptacle for offerings. To rid yourself of negative emotions and feelings, gently blow into an empty cup, mentally emptying yourself of your problems. Then, turn the cup upside down on the altar. This symbolizes your turning your problems over to a higher power to be solved and transformed.

Child—The image of a child symbolizes the future with its potential as yet unrealized, the deeply hidden treasure in the mystic center of each human, or the beginning of a new cycle.

Circle—An ancient symbol, the circle represents the return from multiples to unity, from time to timelessness, from body-obsessed consciousness to the spiritually centered subconscious.

Jung calls the circle the ultimate state of Oneness, for it has no beginning and no end. Engravings of circles and cups can be seen in Paleolithic caves and Neolithic graves. The Gnostics used a drawing of a snake with its tail in its mouth to represent the circle; this symbol was called the ouroboros and it represented the cycles of time, life, the universe, death, and rebirth.

The Native Americans made and still make circular medicine wheels. Permanent circles often marked holy places and sacred sites, such as Stonehenge and the Chinese Temple of Heaven.

To several ancient cultures, the black circle represented the sun god during his nightly passage through the Underworld. Sometimes, instead of the sun god, it symbolized his dark twin brother, a secret, very wise god who held knowledge about all worlds.

Modern Wiccans and magicians draw a circle about their ritual area to symbolize protection from negative astral forces and to represent moving beyond the material world's vibrations.

Clover or trefoil—Long before Christianity arose, the clover, or any three-leafed plant, was an emblem of the Triple Goddess; among Christians, it became the symbol of the Trinity. All trinity symbols date back to the time of the Goddess religions when they represented the Maiden, Mother, and Crone aspects of the Goddess. As far back as the civilization in the Indus Valley (c. 2500–1700 B.C.E.), the trefoil emblem signified a triple deity.

Cobweb—Associated with the Fate goddesses and weaving, the cobweb is the spiral shape of the creative matrix that leads inward to the center where matter is destroyed before being reformed. Minerva, Athena, and Spider Woman are associated with spiders and cobwebs.

Column, tree, ladder, obelisk—Symbolic of the connection between heaven and earth, or gods and mortals, this emblem has been pictured as a ladder, column, World Tree, sacred mountain, obelisk of the sun god, or tent pole of the shamans. It is much the same symbol as the bridge. When in pairs, the columns signify the balancing of opposing forces.

Cornucopia—This horn of plenty, usually filled with fruits and vegetables, symbolizes strength, abundance, and prosperity.

Crescent—The crescent is a lunar and Goddess symbol. It represents the world of changing forms that goes through a cycle to repeat itself endlessly.

Cromlech—Whether part of a circle of monolithic stones or standing alone, the cromlech stands for fertility, health, and spiritual enlightenment. A cromlech is an arrangement of stones, consisting of a cap stone on top of surrounding stones.

Cross—Now a Christian symbol, the cross is actually a very ancient symbol, meaning much the same as the column. However, the crosspiece of this emblem signifies the balance of the four elements. The cross was associated with the Phoenician goddess Astarte, the Greek deities Artemis and Aphrodite, and the Aztec goddess of rain.

Crown—In cultures as far apart as India and northern Europe, the crown symbolized the sacred marriage between the Goddess and Her consort. This emblem signifies light, achievement, success, and spiritual enlightenment.

Cube—The three-dimensional equivalent of the square, this symbol represents the material world of the four elements. It is also associated with stability. A box with a lid can be a cube into which you place your requests on slips of paper.

Curl, loop, rope—As with the knot, this emblem means binding and unbinding, especially in a magical or spiritual sense.

Curtain, veil—The veil represents the ethereal door between the worlds of matter and spirit. Seven veils were associated with the goddesses Ishtar and Isis.

Dice—These represent gambling with the Fates; taking chances.

Disk—A sun emblem, the disk symbolizes matter in a state of transformation. Associated with the sun, the disk also signifies celestial perfection.

Door, gate, portal—Any door signifies the entrance to the path leading to spirit, an initiation, or the opening of a new talent or way of life. In addition, the door represents the ability to pass from the earth to the astral plane, from one cycle of life to another, or to another level of spiritual knowledge. Similar to circles, doors also symbolize a separation of the physical and the sacred, signaling to the subconscious mind that a mindset transition must be made. The two-faced Roman god Janus, deity of the past and the future, ruled over doorways of all kinds. Altars were frequently placed near doors in ancient Greece, Rome, Assyria, and Mexico.

Drum—This instrument symbolizes divine ecstasy in ritual. In Africa, the drum is associated with the heart, while other cultures that practice any form of shamanism believe it is a mediator between earth and heaven.

Dwarf—The personification of forces that remain outside the realm of consciousness, this figure represents the guardian of the threshold between the conscious and subconscious minds, and the guardian who protects us from being exposed to more than we can understand or assimilate.

Ear of corn—Associated with many harvest deities, including Ceres and Demeter, an ear of corn represents the disintegration of life followed by rebirth. It also symbolizes the germination and growth of ideas. Maize or grains of corn represent prosperity and fertility.

Egg—Eggs dyed red were an important part of early Goddess worship and ritual, especially in spring. In ancient Egypt, the hieroglyph of an egg represented the potential seed of rebirth. Several creation myths tell the story of the World Egg. This symbol signifies immortality and the potential for life renewal.

Eye—Thousands of statues of the Eye Goddess have been excavated from third-millennium Sumer, where this aspect of the Goddess was very sacred. In Egypt, the eye was associated primarily with the god Horus. The eye is associated with intelligence, spiritual light, intuition, and truth that cannot be hidden. It also represents judgment by the Goddess.

Fan—Femininity, intuition, and change. The fan is an emblem of the Chinese deity Chung-Li Chuan, one of the Eight Chinese Immortals.

Feather, plume—In Egypt, the feather of truth was associated with the goddess Maat. It represents faith, contemplation, and reincarnating souls. Many goddesses, including Juno, were associated with feathers, which represent change.

Flower—Flowers are usually connected with spring and rebirth or renewal. For a more complete explanation of flowers, read the Flowers chart.

Fountain—The main portion of the fountain is associated in a minor way with the World Tree, while the flowing water represents the life force within all things. The fountain symbolizes blessings, wisdom, purification, renewal, and comfort arising from the Divine Center.

Geode—A womb symbol similar to the cave.

Globe, sphere—Representing the world soul and the human soul, the globe or sphere symbolizes wholeness. If it is depicted with wings, it represents spiritual evolution.

Goblet—The same as the chalice and cauldron.

Grain, wheat, corn—This emblem represents life and the sustaining of it, and the harvest.

Grapes—Associated with such gods as Dionysus, grapes represent fertility and sacrifice.

Hand—Handprints are among the first symbols found in ancient, sacred Paleolithic caves. There, red marks of individual hands are found among wavy lines for water and crescent-shaped horns of fertility. In the shrines of matriarchal Catal Huyuk in seventh-millennium Anatolia, handprints, along with butterflies, bees, and the heads of bulls, decorate the walls. In Catal Huyuk, the hand probably represented the hand of the Goddess and action or manifestation, while in ancient Egypt, when combined with an eye, it signified clairvoyant action. In present Islamic cultures, the hand is still sacred and symbolizes protection, power, and strength.

Harp—Similar to the World Tree or mystic ladder, the harp is another symbol of the bridge between heaven and earth.

Heart—The ancient Egyptians believed that thoughts and morals arose from the heart, the center of physical life and a symbol of eternity. Thus, this symbol represents moral judgment, and pure, true love.

Hexagram or six-pointed star—The six-pointed star is composed of two overlapping triangles oriented in opposite directions, and is found around the world. It is also known as the Seal of Solomon, David's Shield, or the Star of David (in Judaism). The hexagram represents the combination of male and female.

Honey—To the Greek Orphists, honey was a symbol of wisdom. In India, it symbolizes the higher self.

Horns—Originally a fertility and lunar symbol, to early cultures horns also represented strength, power, and prosperity. The Egyptian hieroglyph of the horn signified elevation, prestige, and glory. The word horned may be derived from the Assyro-Babylonian *garnu* or the Phoenician words *geren, qarnuim,* or *kerenos*. The horned Apollo Karnaios resembles the horned Celtic god Cernunnos.

Horseshoe—Originally a symbol of the Goddess, the horseshoe represents the ending of one cycle and the beginning of another.

Hourglass—This emblem symbolizes the cycle and connection between the upper (spiritual) and lower (physical) worlds; creation and destruction.

Jar, urn—Long a sacred object in many cultures, a pot or jar represents the universal womb of the Goddess and the Oneness that proceeds from the Great Mother. It symbolizes the potential for transforming anything placed inside it. In China, the jar represents good luck. Isis was frequently portrayed with a jar about her neck, just as the Hindu goddess Kali was shown with pots and jars.

Many sacred ceremonies involved the use of water jars to signify the presence of the deities. These ceremonies included the Osirian Mysteries of Egypt, the Babylonian rites of the god Nabu, the Cabirian Mysteries for Demeter and Cabirius, and the Greek festival of Anthesteria for Dionysus.

Keys—This symbol is associated with many deities from a variety of cultures. Hecate and Persephone held the keys to the Underworld and the universe. Athena was said to control the key to the city of Athens. The Babylonian god Marduk is said to have made the keys to heaven and hell that only Ishtar could use. In Rome, women in labor were given keys to hold for an easy childbirth. The Egyptian god Serapis was believed to have the keys to both the earth and the sea. Ancient spiritual mysteries speak of keys as the symbol of knowledge, a task to be performed, or a successful quest or spiritual journey. Keys are still used as a symbol of warding off evil spirits, and represent the means of solving a mystery or performing a task. They are also symbolic of locking and unlocking, or binding and loosening.

Knife—While the sword symbolizes spiritual heights, the knife represents vengeance, death, and sacrifice; it also alludes to the means to end a cycle.

Knot—The knot has two meanings: unity, stopping progress, or binding up energies when it is tied, but also releasing energy when untied. It is closely associated with weaving and the woven web of life. This symbol, with its weaving connotations, was connected with the Greek Fate goddesses and the Norse Norns.

In ancient Egypt, Isis was said to loosen or bind the knot of life, while Hathor wore a *menat*, the knotted headband or necklace. All the Egyptian holy mysteries were called "she-knots." The knot can be found in the Egyptian circle of eternity, the loop of the ankh, and the cartouche that circles the name of a pharaoh. Priestesses of the Goddess in Crete wore a knot of hair at the back of their heads and hung a knot of cloth at the entrance to the shrines.

In Rome, it was forbidden for anyone to wear anything knotted or tied within the precinct of Juno, who was the goddess of childbirth; knots were thought to cause a difficult birth. Muslims will not wear knots when they take their pilgrimage to Mecca. According to rabbinical law, Jews are not to tie knots on the Sabbath. One of the Chinese emblems of good luck is the Buddhist "endless knot" of longevity. Among the

Celts, the knot was a protective device to trap negative or evil energies.

Tie knots in string or yarn to bind up negative energy. Or use intricate drawings of knotwork to release energy when it is needed.

Labyrinth—The labyrinth takes its name from the ancient Minoan labrys, or double ax. However, the idea and use of the labyrinth in drawings goes back much further than Crete. Such designs are found on the walls of Paleolithic caves, where the ritual participants had to crawl through narrow openings and traverse narrow passageways to reach the sacred center of the cave itself. This symbol represents the spiritual path leading back to the Divine Center, and regeneration through the Goddess by the process of initiative rebirth. Focus on a drawing of a labyrinth while tracing the path with your finger. This will draw you toward the spiritual center of your being.

Labrys, double ax—A Goddess and moon symbol widely used in Minoan Crete, the labrys was sacred as a ritual tool. It was also a sacred image of the Amazons, who used it both in battle and as a ritual tool. It symbolizes the renewing of the life cycle and the soul through sacrifice, or death and regeneration.

Lamp—This emblem symbolizes spiritual intelligence and enlightenment. The Hermit of the tarot cards is shown holding a lamp or lantern, denoting his offering of guidance and higher instruction. Deities associated with the lamp were Juno Lucina and Diana Lucifera.

Leaf—To the Chinese, the leaf means happiness.

Mask—In ancient times, the mask was worn during Mystery rituals to signify the spiritual metamorphosis conferred by the rite itself. This emblem represents secrecy, hidden meanings, and shapeshifting.

Mirror—A Goddess and moon symbol whose meanings include revealing the truth, intuition and the psychic realm, and the imagination. Mirrors were also known as soul-catchers or soul-carriers; Celtic women were buried with their mirrors that they believed carried their souls.

Moon—Originally a symbol of many goddesses and a few gods, the moon later came to symbolize the rhythm of life and the universe, the passage of time, and the power of rebirth. The moon represents creation, ripeness, cycles of life, spiritual disciplines, and initiations.

Necklace—At one time a sexual symbol of the completeness of the Goddess, the threaded, beaded necklace later came to mean the unity of diversity, or the continuity of the past lives of a human. The goddesses Freyja and Ishtar wore special necklaces.

Nest—This symbol represents the foundation or beginning of a life, event, or path.

Oar—This mundane object represents action, controlling the direction life is taking, and stability within an unstable situation.

Obelisk—Primarily a symbol of ancient Egypt, the obelisk was an emblem of the sun god and considered to be a solidified ray of the sun. Physically, it was a slender, four-sided, tapering column that could be hundreds of feet high. Obelisks frequently stood beside the doors of temples. The door to the temple of the goddess Astarte at Byblos was flanked by a pair of obelisks.

Palace, castle—This emblem represents the sacred place within, or the Divine Center.

Papyri, book—Whether a rolled scroll or a bound book, this symbol means knowledge and an unfolding of the Akashic Records. These Records are a spiritual compilation of all the lives of every person.

Peach—To the Asians, the peach symbolizes immortality.

Pearl—Considered one of the eight Chinese emblems, the pearl signifies the sacred center. To Muslims, it represents heaven or paradise.

Pentacle, pentagram—A pentacle is a five-pointed star, once the symbol of all things feminine and the great Earth Mother. In Egyptian hieroglyphs, it means to "rise up" or "cause to arise," and it was associated with both Isis and Nephthys. The pentacle was also a symbol of the Babylonian Ishtar and the Celtic Morrigan. To the Gnostics, it represented the sacred number five, while for Pythagoreans it meant harmony of the body and mind. The five-pointed star was also associated with the Virgin Mary in her aspect of Stella Maris (Star of the Sea). This symbol represents the repulsion of evil, or protection.

Pine cone—A product of the pine tree, which symbolizes immortality, the cone represents psychic oneness. It was one of the symbols of both Astarte in ancient Byblos and the sacrificed savior Attis. The sacred wand of Dionysus, called the *thyrsus*, was tipped with a pine cone, as was that of the Roman Bacchus.

Plait, braid—Long associated with rope and knots, the braid represents the intertwining of relationships or creative matter.

Pomegranate—The Greek Underworld goddess Persephone was linked with the pomegranate, thus giving it the meaning of the dead lying in sleep before rebirth. Deities associated with this fruit were Persephone, Dionysus, Adonis, Attis, and the Crone aspect of the Goddess.

Pumpkin—An emblem of Li T'ieh-Kuai, one of the Chinese Immortals, the pumpkin represents a link between two worlds. It can also mean an upheaval in the usual order.

Pyramid—Similar in meaning to the triangle, the pyramid is actually a hollow mountain. It symbolizes rebirth, regeneration, and creation.

Rainbow—Similar to the bridge, ladder, and obelisk, the rainbow represents the connection between the earth and the sky, or the mundane world and the sacred. The Greek goddess Iris carried messages from the gods to humans on this celestial bridge. In the Middle East, the rainbow symbolized the veils of Ishtar and, in the Far East, the illusive veils of Maya. Among the Pueblo and Navajo Indians, the rainbow was known as the road of the spirits and gods.

Ring—Similar to the circle, the ring represents continuity and wholeness. When associated with the Fates, it symbolizes the eternally repeated cycles of time.

Scales—First seen in Chaldean carvings, the scales symbolize justice, cause and effect, and the divine assessment of a life. Deities associated with this emblem were Maat and Astraea.

Scepter—Related to the magic wand, the thunderbolt, the phallus, and Thor's hammer, the scepter represents fertility, purification, and the ability and willpower to make changes.

Scissors—A symbol of both life and death, scissors were associated with the Fates and other deities who ruled over the length of life.

Scythe—Connected with the god Saturn and with the moon, the scythe represents reaping the harvest, or the harvest when the life-path is finished.

Sheaf, bundle—Related to knots, the sheaf symbolizes unification and strength, but also limitation because of the binding.

Shell—To Chinese Buddhists, the shell is one of the eight emblems of good luck. It is related to the moon, the sea, and all sea deities. The spiral form of the shell represents the life force moving toward the sacred center.

Shield—Protection, identity.

Ship—The journey through physical life, or the inner, spiritual journey.

Sieve—Sorting out, purifying, discarding the useless.

Spiral—Connected with both the snake and the labyrinth, the spiral is an ancient sacred symbol. Spirals appear on Paleolithic sacred sites and objects and represent the awesome powers of death and rebirth, a process Pagans and Zirceans believe is held only by the Goddess. The spiral signifies the unfolding of potent, creative energy.

Square—Symbolic of the four elements, the square represents order and direction. It is considered to be of feminine nature with strong connections to the earth. Egyptian hieroglyphs used the square to mean achievement. Carl Jung believed this symbol signified the unachieved state of inner unity. The square represents definition, stability, and firmness.

Staff—Support, authority.

Star—To many cultures, the star signified the dead; in Judaism it is believed that each star has a guardian angel. The Aztecs said that stars were the regenerated spirits of fallen or sacrificed warriors. The star symbolizes spirit shining in the darkness of the labyrinth and a beacon to guide the pilgrim on the journey through the subconscious.

Swastika—Although not likely to appeal to most people today, this symbol had a long history of deep, spiritual meaning before it was perverted by the Nazis. The name actually comes from the Sanskrit words *su*, "good," and *asti*, "being." Connected with both the sun and the moon, it signifies movement and regenerative power.

Sword—Strength, defense.

Thunderbolts—Celestial fire, illumination, chance, destiny; associated with Zeus, Jupiter, Shiva, Pyerun, and Thor.

Tower—Rising above the physical; ascent of the spirit.

Triangle—This was an early symbol of the feminine principle. In Paleolithic times, skulls were often buried under triangular rocks, representing the Goddess's power of rebirth. For the Pythagoreans, the Greek letter delta (a triangle) symbolized cosmic birth. The triangle was associated with the Hindu goddess Durga, the Celtic Triple Goddess, the Greek Moerae, the Nordic Norns, and the triple Roman Fortunae. The triangle symbolizes body, mind, and spirit, and therefore represents the Triple Goddess.

Trumpet—Fame and glory; warning; Elements of Fire and Air.

Vase—An ancient symbol of repose, life, and fertility, vases with breasts have been dated back to the sixth millennium B.C.E. During rituals, these breast-vases were filled with a liquid that was sprinkled through the nipples onto the offering and worshippers. The Chinese goddess Kuan Yin often holds a vase in one hand.

Water—Primal matter, universal possibilities.

Wheel—The wheel differs from the circle in that it has spokes that divide it. To the Romans, the wheel was an emblem of the goddess Fortuna, who ruled the fate or changing fortunes of humans. The wheel of the Hindu goddess Kali is the wheel of karma. The Buddhists call the wheel the Holy Wheel of Life, while the Celts used an eight-spoked wheel to represent their sacred year with its eight sacred festivals. Today, the wheel is commonly seen as one of the Major Arcana cards in tarot decks, where it represents the changing cycles of fortune. Frequently, the wheel is a solar symbol and connected with sun gods. It signifies spiritual advancement or regression, and the progression of karma, which is payment of good and evil done in a life.

Wings—In many ancient carvings and drawings, wings denoted the divine and were added to figures of deities or sacred objects. Wings represent ideas, thoughts, spirituality, imagination, mobility, and enlightenment.

Yin/Yang Symbol—This Asian symbol is a circle divided into half-white and half-black by a curving S. It represents perfect balance.

COLORS AND ELEMENTS

Most world cultures recognized the elements of Earth, Air, Fire, and Water, and used their colors and powers in magical and spiritual practices. These elements were usually connected with the cardinal directions—north, east, south, and west. The elements are forces and energies that make up the universe and everything in it. They also influence human personalities and are employed in the practice of magic. When used singularly, the proper elemental color is placed in the appropriate direction. When used all together, the elemental colors are arranged in the appropriate directions at the edge of a sacred circle.

The Celts, particularly those in Scotland, used red in the east for the rising sun, white in the south for noon, gray in the west for twilight, and black in the north for midnight. In Scotland, they were called the Four Airts or Airs and were based on the prevailing winds in Britain. The Scottish Gaelic words for the cardinal directions were *aiet*, east; *deas*, south; *iar*, west; and *tuath*, north. The Druids said that the center was ruled by *nyu*, or spirit. In later Western cultures the correspondences became Air, yellow, east; Fire, red, south; Water, blue, west; Earth, dark green or black, north; and Spirit, white, center.

In this tradition, the east represents knowledge, harmony, the intellect and ideas, freedom, revealing the truth, finding lost things, travel, and psychic abilities. The south signifies change, perception, spiritual illumination, cleansing, sexuality, energy, authority, healing, and purification. The west is associated with the emotions, healing, plants, communion with the spiritual realm, purification, the subconscious mind, love, friendships, marriage, fertility, happiness, dreams, and the psychic on an emotional level. The north represents endurance, responsibility, stability, thoroughness, and purpose in life. The center represents enlightenment, finding your life path, spiritual knowledge, and seeing and understanding karmic paths in life.

In other cultures, both placement and choice of color differed. The Hindus used what are called *tattwas* symbols to represent the elements. A yellow square represented north and Earth; a silver crescent, west and Water; a blue circle, east and Air; a red triangle, south and Fire; and a black or indigo ovoid, the center and Spirit.

In the Western Hemisphere, the native peoples had many differing traditions about colors. The ancient Mayas, for example, used red in the east, yellow in the south, black in the west, and white in the north. Other ancient Mexican cultures had a different classification—green and Water in the east, blue and

Air in the south, yellow and Earth in the west, red and Fire in the north, and many colors together in the center.

The Native American tribes further north had still different groupings of colors. The Navajos used white in the east, blue in the south, yellow in the west, and black in the north, while the Zuni had yellow in the east, red in the south, blue in the west, white in the north, and all colors in the center. However, the Cheyenne of the Plains believed that red was in the east, yellow in the south, white or blue in the west, and black in the north. Other Plains tribes used yellow in the east with the totem animal eagle; red in the south with mouse; black in the west with bear; and white in the north with buffalo.

Colors, separate from the elements, have also played an important part in the religion and magic of many cultures. Today, color is primarily used in candle burning and for the cloth that is sometimes spread over the altar or shelf.

Traditional Colors

Black—This color absorbs and removes anything negative. It is used for reversing or binding negative forces; releasing, breaking up blockages, and unsticking stagnant situations. One of the most powerful colors available, black represents protection, mystery, and the ability to become "invisible." According to Marija Gimbutas, Neolithic cultures thought black to be the color of fertility; the deep, damp, nurturing earth; the hidden cauldron of primordial matter.

Blue—To the Navajo, blue is the fertile, nurturing power of the earth, while in Tibetan Buddhism, it represents both emptiness and potential. The hue of this color plays an important part in its use. *Light blue*—truth, inspiration, wisdom, healing, understanding, good health, inner peace, patience, and harmony. *Royal blue*—loyalty, group success, occult knowledge, and expansion.

Brown—This color can be used to attract money and establish financial success. It is also used for balance, concentration, basic material needs, grounding, and communication with nature spirits. To some cultures, brown represents the cycle of life, running from the brown earth in the spring to the withered vegetation in the autumn. To the ancient Romans, this color symbolized humility.

Gold or clear light yellow—Great good fortune, intuition, understanding, fast luck if circumstances are out of your control, and contacting higher influences. It is also useful for happiness, money, and gaining knowledge.

Gray—A neutral color, it symbolizes the art of meditation and the state of existence just before rebirth.

Green—This color can bring a fresh outlook on life or can balance an unstable situation. It also aids with abundance, fertility, good fortune, generosity, success, renewal, marriage, balance, and healing. In ancient Egypt, this color represented both life and death, and was associated with the god Osiris. To the Romans, green belonged to the goddess Venus and love; for many centuries, brides wore green.

Indigo—This shade is a purplish blue that is almost black. Use it for meditation, balancing out karma, and neutralizing another's magic. It also is useful to stop gossip, lies, and undesirable competition.

Magenta—This is a very dark but clear red with a deep purple tint. This color has a very high vibrational frequency that makes things happen fast. It is best to burn a magenta candle together with other colors. Use it for quick changes, spiritual healing, and exorcism.

Orange—A powerful color, use orange only if you are prepared to face major changes. It is good for encouragement, stimulation, sudden changes, prosperity, creativity, success, energy, and mental agility.

Pink—This color represents the purest form of true love and friendship. It is helpful with romance, spiritual awakening, healing, and family love. It helps to banish hatred, depression, and negativity.

Purple or violet—Since purple is such a powerful hue, use it with caution. It aids with success, higher psychic ability, wisdom, progress, deliberate action, protection, spirit contact, breaking bad luck, driving away evil, divination, success in court cases, business success, and influencing people who have power over you. This color was long associated with priests and priestesses.

Red—Use red for energy, strength, sexual potency, courage, willpower, good health, and to protect against psychic attack. Considered to be a sacred color all over the world, for millennia, red was associated with life, the womb, birth, and blood. Only with the rise of patriarchal cultures did red become a symbol of combat and the gods of war. To the Hindus, red belongs to the goddess Lakshmi, deity of good luck and prosperity.

Silver or clear light gray—Victory, stability, help with meditation, developing psychic abilities, neutralizing any situation, and repelling destructive forces.

White—A highly balanced spiritual color, white helps with spirituality, truth, wholeness, balancing the aura, pregnancy and birth, raising the vibrations, and destroying negative energies. Through the Neolithic period, white was considered the color of death and clean-picked bones. In Asia, white is still the color of mourning. However, in the West, by the time of the Greek states, white had become associated with purity and innocence. In ancient Egypt, white was one of the colors of the cycle of life, along with black, red, and green. The Druids wore white robes, representing their spiritual connection with the Otherworld. Thus, this color also symbolizes initiation, spiritual light, and mystical knowledge.

Yellow—The intellect, imagination, creativity, confidence, attraction, concentration, inspiration, mental clarity, knowledge, commerce, medicine, and healing. To several Native American tribes, yellow represents reproduction and growth. However, Buddhism uses this color for robes to symbolize renunciation of worldly matters.

Asian Colors

The Chinese have five elements—Wood, Fire, Earth, Metal, and Water. Their interpretation of color meanings is also different from those in the West. They placed green in the east for spring and the element of Wood; red in the south for Fire and summer; white in the west for Metal and autumn, black in the north for Water and winter; and yellow in the center for Earth.

With *feng shui* (the art of placement) becoming so popular, many people will be interested in utilizing Asian colors on their altars.

Black—The color of the element of Water, winter, and the north. Use with great caution when combining it with red. Deception, penance.

Blue—Self-cultivation, consideration, and thoughtfulness.

Gold—One of the colors of the element of Metal, autumn, and the west. A very fortunate color, said to attract success, wealth, strength, and a good reputation.

Gray—Travel and helpful people.

Green—The color of the element of Wood, spring, and the east. Rebirth, new growth, family, harmony, health, peace, posterity, and longevity.

Pink—Marriage.

Purple or violet—Truth and spiritual growth. It is a visionary color.

Red—The color of the element of Fire, summer, and the south. Happiness, good fortune, a long and stable marriage, prosperity, and spiritual blessings.

White—One of the colors of the element of Metal, autumn, and the west. Children, helpful people, marriage, mourning, peace, purity, and travel.

Yellow—The color of the element of Earth and the center. Blessings, developing the intuition; great wisdom, ambition, and guarding against evil.

STONES

Gemstones and minerals have been used by most world cultures for centuries for their healing and magical properties. They were employed in ritual worship and worn as talismans. Talismans are actually a form of portable altar that we carry with us. The following list by no means describes all the known and used stones.

Agate—Strength and courage. It also balances energies. *Blue Lace Agate* can remove blockages from the nervous system and promote calmness. *Moss Agate* is an opener for the crown and brow chakras, thus connecting the physical with the spiritual. It can also protect the aura, cleanse the environment, and help one to balance logic with intuition. It can be used to attract enlightenment and luck, while helping to open psychic abilities and facilitate contact with spiritual guides. *Brown Agate* helps one to become grounded when one's energies and emotions are flying everywhere. *Orange and Brown Agate* also aids in grounding and stabilizing.

Amber—This fossilized resin has a wide range of magical uses. By helping to stabilize brainwave patterns, it can change negativity to positivity, both in thoughts and surrounding vibrations. It also calms, protects, repels psychic attack, gently revitalizes, and aids in releasing karmic problems and influences.

Amethyst—A major stabilizing and grounding stone, it balances the aura and cleanses it. It also improves meditation and breaks negative patterns. On the spiritual level, amethyst aids in developing psychic abilities and helps to open spiritual dimensions.

Bloodstone—Although not a stone of great beauty, bloodstone brings renewal and harmony, and enhances talents and creativity. It is also valuable when attempting to contact deceased ancestors.

Carnelian—This reddish orange stone raises the mood, aids in seeing into the past, grounds, and protects. It is also helpful in stabilizing the energy in an atmosphere and repelling psychic attacks or ghosts.

Chrysocolla—Comparable to lapis lazuli, this stone can soothe grief, ease tension and heartache, give inner strength, and balance the emotions.

Chrysoprase—Green in color, this stone can balance the attitudes, heal heartache and old traumas, and help one to accept one's self.

Fluorite—The green-colored stone helps with concentration, gives the ability to see through illusions, and calms the nervous system. The purple-colored fluorite aids in psychic development; grounds, calms, and protects.

Garnet—Red garnet draws earth energy. It can attract a compatible mate, protect against negatives, give courage, and regenerate.

Hematite—This gray-black stone is useful for grounding, calming, reducing stress, and dispelling negativity.

Lapis lazuli—Known and used for centuries, this stone has many uses. It can be used to gain wisdom in understanding spiritual mysteries, bring success in relationships, protect from psychic attack, release past pain, and raise the mood.

Malachite—A green stone, it helps to change situations, release negative experiences, inspire hope, create an unobstructed path to goals, and prevent attack by negative vibrations. It also connects the physical plane to the spiritual.

Obsidian—Black obsidian is very useful in grounding, calming, protecting, shielding from negative thoughtforms, and collecting scattered energy. It can also aid in making psychic contact and dealing with past lives.

Onyx—Black onyx will absorb negativity, protect, reduce stress, banish grief, enhance self-control, and draw good fortune.

Pyrite—This glittering, gold-colored stone aids the memory and intellect, protects from all negativity, and grounds the energies.

Quartz crystal—A very powerful, all-healing, transpersonal stone, clear quartz crystal cleanses the atmosphere, helps with clear thinking, aids in contacting spirit guides, enhances psychic abilities, energizes, harmonizes, and dispels negativity.

Rose quartz—A pink stone connected with the heart and love, it balances, relieves depression, and rejuvenates. It is also helpful for acceptance, forgiveness, learning self-love, healing emotional pain, and attaining inner peace.

Tiger's eye—This stone, with its golden brown color, aids in recognizing karmic ties, manifesting ideas into reality, protecting, balancing, and stimulating wealth.

Tourmaline—All colors of tourmaline can inspire, balance the energies, and clear the aura. *Green tourmaline*, also called *verdelite*, transforms negative energy into positive, draws prosperity and creativity, calms fears, attracts love, and dispels fear. *Watermelon tourmaline* helps to heal past emotional scars, stabilizes, attracts love, and protects.

Turquoise—A powerful stone and master healer, it protects, calms, draws prosperity and good luck, absorbs negativity, and increases psychic abilities.

TREES

Using the wood, leaves, and fruit products from certain trees can also enhance your altar energies. Most trees were sacred to specific deities in one culture or another. Even today, these trees are valued for their scents, their energy patterns, and their magical qualities. Acorns and pine cones can be used to decorate the altar during certain seasons of the year, as well as for specific purposes. Clusters of leaves make eye-pleasing bouquets, particularly in the autumn, with their variety of colors and textures. Wood can be made into wands or purchased in the form of boxes or other objects.

Apple—In Greek legend, Gaea, the Earth Mother, gave an apple and its tree to the goddess Hera as a wedding gift. When an apple is cut crosswise, a five-pointed star, symbol of many goddesses, is seen inside. This fruit symbolized immortality to the Norse and the Greeks, and earthly desires to the Christians. It represents beauty, goodness, renewal, death, and rebirth. Use it to represent the ending of one cycle of life and the beginning of another.

Ash—This tree has been considered sacred by several ancient cultures. Among the Norse, it is associated with

Yggdrasil, the World Tree, which had its roots in the well of wisdom. The Irish Druids fashioned the wood into wands and spear shafts, while in Greece it was considered a tree of the god Poseidon. It symbolizes grandeur and prudence.

Bay—In ancient Greece, the bay tree was sacred to Apollo and often made into crowns or wreaths as rewards. It was believed to ward off evil spirits and protect property. Bay twigs with leaves were used by Roman priests to sprinkle holy water.

Birch—This tree has always been associated with the Goddess. It is a symbol of the returning summer. Sprigs of birch were worn on the Summer Solstice and other ancient holidays.

Cedar—A symbol of immortality and sacred to Osiris, the evergreen cedar was used for coffins in ancient Egypt. The Romans fashioned statues of cedar, and many Native American tribes use it in purifying smudges. To help ground yourself, place the palms of your hands against the ends of cedar needles.

Cherry—The cherry was particularly sacred to Far Eastern cultures, where it was a symbol of immortality. The Chinese goddess Hsi-Wang Mu guarded the celestial cherries that only ripened every one thousand years. Doorway guardians, who warded off evil spirits, were carved of cherry wood. In Japan, Kono-Hana-Sakuya-Hime was goddess of the cherry tree.

Cypress—To the Greeks, cypress was sacred to Underworld deities such as Persephone; they also associated it with

Cronus, Apollo, the healer Asclepius, Cybele, Aphrodite, Artemis, Hera, Athena, and the Fates. The cypress symbolizes death and returning to the abyss of regeneration; the Greeks buried their dead heroes in cypress coffins, and the Egyptians also fashioned cypress into mummy cases. A variety of cypress in Japan, called *hinoki*, is used for Shinto ritual fires.

Elder—Sacred among the Celts, this tree was associated with the White Goddess and the Summer Solstice. Wands of elder wood can drive out negativity and evil spirits.

Elm—This tree symbolizes dignity.

Fig—Called the "fruit of heaven," the fig tree has been sacred throughout the Middle East as a symbol of life and plenty. It was sacred to the Roman goddess Juno.

Fir—Burning the needles of this evergreen tree will cleanse the atmosphere and bless your entire house.

Hawthorn—This tree has long been associated with fairies and Otherworld beings. It is considered unlucky to bring the flowers into the house except on May 1. It symbolizes hope.

Hazel—The Druids taught that this tree symbolized wisdom, knowledge, poetry, fire, beauty, and fertility. They ate its nuts to gain inspiration and eloquence.

Holly—Considered a lucky tree, holly is said to ward off evil spirits. The ancient Persian followers of Zoroaster made an infusion of holly leaves and berries for their religious rituals. The Druids believed it to be sacred as a plant symbolizing death and regeneration, while the Norse thought it sacred to the Underworld goddess Hel, who ruled over the dead. In both the Celtic and Norse cultures, holly was used in celebrations at Winter Solstice and hung in the homes of common people as protection against evil spirits. Holly was also given as a friendship gift during the Roman Saturnalia in December.

Juniper—This was a sacred tree to the Celtic Druids, who burned juniper berries and thyme as an incense. It symbolizes protection.

Mistletoe—This parasitic plant, which grows primarily on oaks, has been held as sacred throughout ancient European cultures. It was considered a tree by the Druids, who cut it with great ceremony by using a golden sickle. Both the Greeks and Romans connected it with the Underworld. Its power of death followed by rebirth is shown in the Norse myth when the god Baldur was slain by an arrow of mistletoe and was subsequently reborn. Take care using this plant, as the berries are poisonous to both animals and humans. Nevertheless, mistletoe symbolizes the sweetness of kisses and affection.

Oak—Considered the most sacred of all trees in Europe and the Mediterranean, the Greeks said it was the first tree with roots that ran down into the Underworld. Because of its magical qualities of strength, long life, endurance, and immortality, oak groves in the oracular shrine of Dodona were sacred to

Zeus and to prophecy. The Roman goddess Diana had a shrine in a great forest at Nemi, where a perpetual fire of oak wood was kept burning; her priest, called King of the Wood, ruled there. The Celts worshipped in oak groves and used acorns in their prophesying. Oak was sacred to the Norse god Thor because lightning, caused by his mighty hammer, frequently struck oak trees. Oak was also sacred to Cybele, Jupiter, and Herne the Hunter. As late as the nineteenth century in England, Christians often gathered under "Gospel Oaks" to hold their meetings. This tree symbolizes courage and hospitality.

Orange—An emblem of fertility in China, it was the custom to give twelve oranges as gifts on the New Year. This conveyed wishing the recipient happiness and prosperity.

Palm—In Egypt, palm fronds were frequently laid on coffins or offered to the goddess Hathor. Among the Greeks and Romans, the palm frond was a symbol of victory. Nike, the Greek goddess of victory, was often portrayed holding a palm branch, and the palm was also sacred to Astarte, Isis, and Aphrodite. The Greek word for palm is the same as that for "phoenix," which ties this tree to the Underworld, death, and rebirth. Carvings from ancient Babylon show the palm tree as the Tree of Life.

Peach—In many Eastern cultures the peach symbolized long life and immortality. At one time, Chinese children wore peach pits as amulets, and peach boughs were hung over doorways for protection.

Pear—Pear wood was often used to carve goddess statues in the early Mediterranean cultures. The pear was sacred to the Greek goddesses Hera and Aphrodite, and to the Roman goddess of vegetation, Pomona. In China, the pear represented longevity.

Pine tree—The pine has religious significance in several Mediterranean and Far Eastern cultures because of its connection with immortality, rebirth, and fertility. It represents the life force in Japan and China. Japanese Shinto shrines and ritual tools are made from pine. In the Mediterranean region, during ancient ceremonies honoring the goddess Cybele, this tree represented the body of her consort Attis, who was annually slain and then reborn. Among the Greeks, Etruscans, and Romans, the pine cone was a symbol of fertility and abundance. This tree was also sacred to Artemis, Aphrodite, and Dionysus, who held a pine cone-tipped wand. Burn pine needles to cleanse and purify your home.

Pomegranate—This fruit was considered sacred to many Mediterranean and Middle Eastern goddesses, such as Astarte, Demeter, Aphrodite, Hera, and Persephone. Because its many seeds represented fertility, the womb, and rebirth, it was used in the Greek Eleusinian Mysteries.

Poplar—A tree of the Earth Goddess and Persephone of the Underworld, poplar was said to have regenerative qualities. Myth says that this tree grew at the entrance to Calypso's cave and that Hercules wore a wreath of its leaves when he traveled into the Underworld. It symbolizes courage.

Rowan—This tree is also known as American Ash in the Western Hemisphere. A tree of the Goddess, rowan is thought to bless the property on which it grows.

Spruce—The Navajo Indians of North America made brushes and wands of spruce for use in their sacred rituals.

Willow—This tree was connected with the moon and water, and had the qualities of both creativity and death. It was sacred to Hecate, Circe, Hera, Persephone, and to Apollo in his aspect of god of poetry and prophecy. The Chinese Kuan Yin is said to use a willow wand to sprinkle the water of life. Many Prairie Indian tribes considered willow to be symbolic of seasonal rebirth. In Ireland, priests, priestesses, and artisans sat in willow groves to gain inspiration.

Yew—This tree has long been associated with Underworld deities and was connected with both immortality and death. It was sacred to the goddess Hecate, who ruled with Persephone and Hades in the Greek Underworld. One of the five magical trees of Ireland, yew symbolized the Triple Goddess in Her death aspect. A sacred tree of the Druids, yew was associated with death, rebirth, and the Winter Solstice. The berries are poisonous, and the tree itself symbolizes sorrow.

HERBS

While today herbs and spices are primarily used in cooking or for their scents, for centuries many were considered to be sacred and were used in rituals and worship ceremonies throughout the world. Herbs may be used on the altar as bouquets, in plant form, or dried and sprinkled over burning coals for incense.

Do not eat herbs unless you are absolutely certain of the effect they will cause on the body.

Basil—In India, basil is still grown near homes and temples as protection. It is sacred to the god Vishnu and the goddess Lakshmi. The Greek Orthodox Church uses basil to make holy water and sets basil in pots around the altar.

Bay Laurel—An herb long associated with deities such as Apollo, bay laurel will stop unwanted interference in your life, and protect you against evil.

Catnip—This herb is associated with the goddesses Bast, Sekhmet, and Freyja. It brings courage, love, and happiness.

Chamomile—Roman chamomile smells like fresh apples. It is associated with gaining a marriage proposal and bringing gambling luck.

Clove—Besides being used to banish evil, cloves are used to build friendships and gain desires.

Dragon's blood—This is actually the powdered resin of a shrub and was once considered to be extremely rare and valuable. It is good for removing hexes and attracting love and money.

Ferns—The Druids classed ferns as sacred trees and gathered the uncurled fronds of male fern at Summer Solstice to use for good luck. All ferns attract fairies and give protection.

Frankincense—This was considered to be one of the most sacred scents by ancient Greeks, Romans, Persians, Babylonians, Assyrians, and Egyptians. It was also one of the Jewish offerings on the Sabbath. Use it for exorcism, protection, and purification.

Garlic—Although garlic is frequently used only in cooking, because of its strong odor many ancient cultures believed it had valuable properties of protection against evil. The Egyptians used it for swearing oaths. It was left as an offering at crossroads to the Greek goddess Hecate, while the Romans ate it for strength and endurance, and assigned it to Mars.

Ginger—Most people connect the smell of this herb with cookies, pies, and pastries. However, its oldest uses are for love, money, success, and power.

Hyssop—This herb's name in Greek means "holy herb."

Hyssop has a long history of being used to cleanse and purify sacred places.

Juniper berries—Traditionally, this shrub was grown near dwellings for protection, particularly against thieves. However, it is also used to attract love and to develop psychic abilities.

Lemon verbena—This plant is helpful in getting rid of unwanted lovers.

Marjoram—A common cooking herb, marjoram helps with protection when soaked together with mint and rosemary, and the water sprinkled about the house.

Mint—The Druids burned mint leaves to cleanse a space.

Mugwort—A sacred herb to the Celtic Druids, this plant is strongest when picked on a full moon or during the Summer Solstice. Rub the leaves on ritual tools to increase their power.

Myrrh—Another sacred herb from ancient times, myrrh aids in purification, protection, and strengthening spirituality.

Nutmeg—The whole nutmeg is traditionally carried for luck in gambling and lotteries, while the powdered form is useful for love, prosperity, and fertility.

Orris root—This root, in powdered form, is sprinkled about to attract the opposite sex.

Patchouli—An herb highly valued by Hindus, patchouli can

break up any spell, bring back a lost love, attract money, and defeat enemies. It is also useful in healing grief.

Parsley—Given to soldiers as a sign of victory, this herb was also thought to be sacred to the dead in both Greece and Rome.

Pine—Pine needles have a clean, refreshing scent and are used for purifying an atmosphere. It was sacred to such deities as Mars.

Rosemary—The modern name of this herb connects it with the Virgin Mary, although it was known and used in the Mediterranean cultures long before Christianity arose. Its name means "dew of the sea." The Greeks associated it with remembrance, and students wore a sprig of rosemary to help improve their memory. The Romans made crowns of rosemary for their household deities and burned it to purify an atmosphere and ward off evil. A symbol of remembrance and fidelity, it is also useful for exorcisms and to keep a lover faithful.

Rue—In Europe during the Middle Ages, rue was strewn on floors for its scent, a custom begun by the Greeks and Romans, who believed it gave protection from evil spirits. The word rue comes from the Greek word *reuo*, which means "set free." Thus, this herb became a Christian symbol for repentance. Among the Druids, rue was used for defense against magical spells. When burned, it starts things moving.

Saffron—This expensive herb, which is the pollen from crocus flowers, was highly prized from the Mediterranean area to Tibet and India. The Greeks and Romans used it for its scent, which was said to be cleansing. When a worshipper brought a gift to a temple in India, they received a dot of saffron paste on the forehead. Because of saffron's association with humility and purity, Buddhist monks dyed their robes the color of saffron.

Sage—A symbol of wisdom and long life to the Romans, this herb was gathered ceremoniously, with a gift of bread and wine left as an offering to the plant. Native Americans use sage for smudging and cleansing.

Saint John's wort—An herb sacred to the Druids, it was worn in Ireland for invincibility and in Scotland as a charm against fairy glamour. Its other magical associations are attracting happiness and healing; courage, love, and protection. It also is said to aid with divination.

Sandalwood—An herb widely used in India, yellow sandalwood is associated with protection, exorcism, and spiritual growth.

Thyme—The name of this herb is derived from the Greek, meaning "to burn a sacrifice." It was considered a holy incense throughout the Mediterranean cultures. However, the Romans believed thyme was an aphrodisiac and offered it to Venus. The Druids used this plant to repel negativity and depression.

In Medieval Europe, thyme was associated with increasing energy and bravery. Used in pillows, it is said to cure nightmares.

OILS

Oils are best used to anoint candles before lighting them. When wishing to attract something, rub the oil on the candle from the wick to the end. When wanting to repel something, rub from the end to the wick. A few drops of an essential oil can also be placed directly on the top of votive candles. If you put a votive candle in a small cast-iron cauldron to burn, drop the oil in the bottom of the cauldron first. This not only allows the scent to be released with the burning candle, but also helps to keep the wax from sticking to the cauldron. Never drink any essential oils.

Amber—Use for happiness and love.

Bayberry—Long associated with prosperity and money, bayberry is also useful in gaining control of a situation.

Bergamot—A spicy oil, it can aid in attracting money, happiness, and optimism.

Carnation—This oil is most helpful in healing spells, for it draws in strength and protection. Legends associate this oil and the flower with Venus and the warrior Ajax.

Cedar—Oil made from the cedar tree will remove hexes, purify, and heal.

Cinnamon—A scent of richness and money, this oil can also be used for purification and to gain energy.

Clove—Basically a healing oil, clove will also stimulate creativity.

Frankincense and myrrh—This combination is valuable for purification, protection, healing, and great spirituality.

Frangipani—Traditionally, this is an oil for attracting love and the perfect mate.

Gardenia—A sweet-smelling oil, gardenia is used for peace, love, healing, harmony, and happiness.

Heliotrope—This oil attracts wealth and gives protection.

Honeysuckle—The oil of this flower both attracts money and strengthens psychic abilities.

Jasmine—Some people believe that only the extremely expensive, pure jasmine oil will attract love, money, and psychic dreams. However, I have found the less expensive oil works just as well. A symbol of sensuality, the name is said to come from the Persian word *Ysmyn*.

Juniper—Use for protection.

Lavender—This flower oil is primarily used for healing and love.

Lilac—Use to ward off evil and to protect.

Lotus—A sacred flower and oil in ancient Egypt and India, this oil brings protection and purification, while promoting spirituality.

Magnolia—This oil is best for establishing a sense of oneness with nature.

Musk—Although primarily used to attract the opposite sex and promote sexual love, musk can also draw in prosperity.

Myrrh—This oil will break hexes, heal, aid psychic development, and protect.

Patchouli—This oil promotes love and purification.

Peppermint—An oil of great energy, it can stimulate creativity and attract money.

Pine—This oil can protect and cleanse.

Rose—An oil of love, rose also cleanses the atmosphere of a room.

Sage—This oil of purification also aids in finding wisdom and truth.

Sandalwood—Primarily an oil of great spirituality and cleansing.

Vanilla—This oil attracts sexual love.

Vetiver—A powerful oil to be used sparingly, it removes hexes, attracts money, and can stimulate love.

Violet—Use this oil to gain luck and love. It also is helpful in finding wisdom to resolve a problem.

Ylang ylang—This is an oil of love and harmony.

FLOWERS

Flowers have been used as offerings to deities and placed in gravesites for millennia, in a wide variety of cultures. In Rome, when the *Lares*, or property guardians, were honored in early December, flowers were placed at all the boundary stones on a piece of property. Certain flowers have long been associated with particular qualities and spiritual meanings. During the Victorian era, the meanings of flowers changed from spiritual to romantic symbols. Flower meanings became a secret code of love, a means of sending nonverbal messages. Many flowers are also considered to be magical herbs. You can use a flower's symbolism to enhance your altars.

Dreams of flowers in general can mean several things. To dream of gathering flowers means a delightful surprise is coming your way. A basket of flowers portends a wedding or birth, while a wreath of flowers represents a new love. A garden symbolizes a spiritual blessing. To smell flowers in a dream is a sign you should grasp an opportunity that will soon present itself.

Alyssum—This flower symbolizes sweet virtue.

Anemone—Also known as the windflower from the Greek *anemos* (wind), tradition says that Aphrodite created this blossom in remembrance of her lover Adonis. The Greeks associated it with Zephyr, god of the west wind, while the Christians believed it sprang up at the foot of the cross from Jesus' blood. It symbolizes abandonment or being forsaken.

Aster—The name of this flower means "star," for it was said to spring from stardust that the goddess Virgo sprinkled on the earth. Known in England as starwort, after 1637, the name changed to Michaelmas daisy. In Europe, tradition says the aster will drive away evil spirits. It symbolizes beginnings that lead to greater things.

Bluebell—In Scotland, this flower is known as Deadmen's Bells. A tradition says that if you hear a bluebell ring, it is a death knell. These flowers are associated with fairies and enchantment. They symbolize constancy.

Buttercup—This wildflower is a symbol of radiance and brightness in a person, or a childlike appreciation of life.

Camellia—Originally from Japan, this flower symbolizes loveliness.

Carnation—The name comes from the Greek *dios* (divine) and *anthos* (flower). The Greeks used carnations, whose name meant divine flower, to make ceremonial crowns. The red blossom symbolizes passion, while the white represents pure devotion.

Cornflower—Also called the Bachelor's Button, this flower

symbolizes gentleness of manner and hope in solitude. Greek tradition says that a centaur was healed by this flower after Hercules shot it with a poisoned arrow. It received its other name, Bachelor's Button, during the Middle Ages in England, when girls tucked a blossom under their aprons to ensnare the bachelor of their choice.

Chrysanthemum—A solar symbol associated with completion and fullness of life, this flower was a traditional autumn offering flower in the Far East, where it was cultivated (in China) for over 2,400 years before being brought to the West. In Italy, chrysanthemums are associated with death. This flower symbolizes truth and hope in dark times.

Daffodil—Giving a daffodil symbolizes chivalry. The name is derived from the Old English *affodyle*, which means "an early arrival." The Romans introduced this flower to Britain.

Dahlia—When the conquistadors came to Mexico, they found that the Aztecs ate dahlia tubers as a treat; the Aztecs called this flower *cocoxochitl*. It represents the instability of perfect physical beauty.

Daisy—The present name of this flower is derived from the Old English *daeges ege*, meaning "day's eye." As a symbol of innocence, the Christians believed it was sacred to Mary Magdalene and St. John.

Foxglove—The name comes from the Old English name *foxes*

glofa, or "fingers of a glove." The ancients thought the markings on the flowers were the fingerprints of fairies and associated this flower with them. The Victorians thought this flower symbolized insincerity. The seeds contain digitalis and are poisonous.

Gardenia—In China, this flower represented feminine grace, subtlety, and artistry, while in the southern states of the U.S., it meant hospitality. At one time it was known as Cape jasmine, because of a species found in South Africa. During the nineteenth century, this flower was frequently worn by gentlemen on their evening jackets. The gardenia symbolizes sweetness.

Gladiolus—At one time this flower, also known as flags, grew wild in the Middle East. One species grows only in the spray of Victoria Falls in Africa. It symbolizes natural grace.

Heather—This flower grows wild in northern England and Scotland and was said to be a traditional fairy food. The red variety symbolizes passion, while the white means protection from passion.

Heliotrope—Although variations of this flower were discovered in Peru in the eighteenth century, one variety had been known in Europe for millennia. It represents devotion.

Hollyhock—Brought to Europe by the Crusaders, this flower was originally grown for the taste of its leaves in food. In the eighteenth century, new strains were brought from China. The name is derived from *holy* plus *hoc* (mallow). It has several meanings—fertility, creation, abundance, and ambition.

Honeysuckle—The botanical name of this flower means "goat flower." Shakespeare mentioned it under the name woodbine. A symbol of plighted troth, this flower is associated with weddings.

Hyacinth—The blue flower symbolizes dedication, while the white one represents admiration. Named after the youth who loved Apollo, hyacinth also represents young love.

Iris—A symbol of reconciliation and joining, the iris was associated with the Greek goddess of the same name. However, the Egyptians knew of this flower long before and carved images of it into the temples at Karnak. In Japan, this flower is known as *ayame*. Louis VII had irises with him during the Second French Crusade in 1147; from this came the name *fleur de Louis* or fleur-de-lis.

Ivy—Although not technically a flower, this plant is listed in Victorian flower codes as symbolizing tenacity. Wear a leaf over your heart to attract a love.

Jasmine—Known in the East as a symbol of good luck and increase, this flower was brought to Europe by Vasco da Gama, the explorer, in the sixteenth century. The Chinese call this plant *yeh-hsi-ming*. Italian brides sometimes wear a sprig of jasmine at weddings. The name is derived from the ancient Persian word *yasmin*. Traditionally, this flower is used in magic for love, money, and to strengthen psychic abilities. It symbolizes elegance.

Lavender—This flower is widely used to scent drawers and clothing, but is also useful in gaining love, money, and helpful spirits. The name comes from the Latin word *lavare*, "to wash." The Romans added a sprig of lavender to the laundry and also placed it between sheets and blankets. A symbol of distrust, this flower was placed in homes to avoid marital discord.

Lilac—Native to Turkey, this flower's name comes from the Arabic *laylak* or the Persian *nylac*, which means blue. The purple flower represents first love, while the white one symbolizes innocence. These flowers were once thought to ward off the Black Death.

Lilies—An ancient seal from the Minoan culture portrays priestesses bearing temple gifts of water lilies and figs. Another seal shows the Goddess descending into a field of lilies where priestesses are dancing. It was sacred to the Cretan goddess Britomartis because of its powerful association with the feminine. The Greeks believed that the lily sprang from Hera's breast milk dropped upon the earth. The Romans called this flower *rosa Junonis*, which means "Juno's rose." The Christians connected it to Mary because it symbolized purity.

Lily of the Valley—This flower is also called Our Lady's Tears and Liriconfancy. In Greece, priestesses to Hera made offerings of lilies of the valley to invoke her presence. It symbolized modesty.

Lotus—Possibly the flower with the oldest spiritual meanings, the lotus was sacred to cultures from ancient Egypt to those of China and Japan. Before Buddhism was brought to China, the lotus represented summer, purity, fertility, spirituality, and creative power.

A symbol of spiritual purity and the sacred center, the opened lotus was considered sacred in both Buddhism and Hinduism. The bud represented fertility and potential.

In ancient Egypt, this flower symbolized the sun and the resurrection of the god Horus. It was so sacred that it is found painted and sculpted on temples and tombs.

In India, the Hindu goddess Lakshmi is connected with the lotus. When associated with Lakshmi, this flower symbolizes the yoni, or womb of creation. Many Hindu deities are portrayed sitting on the lotus, which in this instance represents divinity and spirit.

Marigold—Known also as calendula and pot marigold, the flowers are said to promote psychic dreams. This flower was first called golds in England. Later, when it was used to adorn statues of the Virgin Mary, it became known as Mary's gold. It symbolizes constancy and endurance in love in some sources, while in others, it stands for grief or cruelty.

Orchid—This flower symbolizes luxury and ecstasy.

Pansy—Also called heartsease, one definition of this flower is broken hearts and disappointment in love. However, another definition lists the symbolism as thoughts exchanged between lovers. The name comes from the French word for "thought," as it was believed that this flower could grant telepathic ability.

Peony—Known and revered from the Mediterranean to the Far East, the peony has long been connected to healing and magic. The plant, flower, and seed were used as protection against evil spirits and natural disasters, particularly storms and shipwrecks. According to the Chinese, this highly prized flower was of the yin, or female, principle. Paeon, the Greek physician to the gods and a student of the healer Asclepius, was associated with the peony, which took his name. This flower represents the ability to keep a secret.

Periwinkle—The Italians call this blue flower the "flower of death," while the French know it as the "violet of sorcery" and the Virgin's flower. It is associated with death because of the tradition that the souls of the dead live within the blossoms. It symbolizes a long relationship.

Poppy—Long associated with sleep, forgetting, and rejuvenation, the poppy was an important part of Egyptian funerary rites. Although the Greeks knew of its narcotic, healing properties, they also offered it at shrines to Demeter and Artemis for fertility, and to Persephone in her death aspect. Their god Morpheus, the god of dreams, was said to use poppy wreaths. The red poppy represents consolation; the pink one, sleep; and the white one, time.

Primrose—Another flower associated with fairies, tradition says to lay one on your doorstep so the fairies will bless your house. Climbers in Switzerland carry the flowers to ward off vertigo. It is a symbol of beginning love, birth, and children.

Rose—One of the most meaningful flowers in the West, a single rose primarily represents achievement and perfection. It can also mean the mystic center, the heart and love, spiritual rebirth, and the soul itself. The yellow rose represents home and domestic happiness; the red stands for beauty and passionate love. Sometimes called the flower of light, the white rose symbolizes purity and silence in the West, but death in Asia.

Ancient Greek myth says that the rose and the anemone sprang into being when the blood of Adonis, the beloved of the goddess Aphrodite, was shed on the ground. The rose was also sacred to Athena. Whenever Hecate was shown wearing a garland of roses, it symbolized the beginning of a new cycle of life. When a chariot containing the statue of Cybele was pulled through Rome during a specific ritual, the Romans tossed roses into the conveyance in her honor. Later, the Christians would honor the Virgin Mary with roses in much the same manner. Deities associated with this flower were Aphrodite, Eros, and Venus. The rose has long been used as a magical herb for love and happiness in the home.

Snowdrop—This flower is a symbol of hope and renewal.

Sunflower—A plant sacred to the sun deities, Inca priestesses wore gold replicas of this flower. Sunflower seeds were used as offerings in Inca rituals. The botanical name comes from that of the Greek sun god Helios. It symbolizes adoration.

Sweetpea—Although the botanical name comes from the Greek word for "pea," this plant is poisonous if ingested. This flower represents tenderness and lasting pleasure. Tradition says that this good omen should be presented at weddings to the married couple.

Tulip—This flower is a native to Persia and was brought to Europe in 1559 by a man who saw them in a walled garden in Constantinople. The name comes from the Turkish *tulbent* (turban). Red symbolizes a declaration of love, while yellow means your love is hopeless. Other sources say the tulip is a lucky charm bringing good luck and fame.

Vervain, verbena—Both an herb and a flower, vervain has been held sacred by many cultures that considered it a plant of enchantment and mystery. In Egypt, it was a symbol of the tears of Isis. Greek priests carried it in their robes and used it to cleanse the altars of Zeus. Celtic Druids and ancient Persians believed that vervain not only purified, but also helped with visions and divination. Christian churches used it to make holy water. As one of the most sacred of Celtic herbs, vervain was placed on altars as an offering. Other names for this herb are verbena and holy herb. Burn it to repel psychic attack. Other uses are for purification, to attract wealth, and to find love.

Violet—Used in ancient love philters, this flower symbolizes faithfulness, modesty, and a steady love.

Yarrow—This flower has been known and used for millennia in religious rituals. The earliest archaeological finding of yarrow pollen was in Neanderthal graves. It has always been associated with healing and the stopping of bleeding. The Celtic Druids used yarrow in many of their ceremonies, as well as for healing. The name is derived from the Anglo-Saxon *gearwe*, which means "to prepare." One Chinese method of divination originally used fifty stalks of dried yarrow. Presented to a new bride, yarrow is said to bring happiness. Wear it to break spells and to protect.

Zinnia—This flower symbolizes thoughts of absent friends. In 1519, when the conquistadors were exploring Mexico, they found zinnias, which they called *mal de ojos*.

DEITIES

The following lists of ancient deities give the esoteric meanings connected with these archetypal figures of power. These major deities are divided according to their country or area of origin and usage. You may wish to choose a goddess or god to whom you are attracted and who portrays the magical and spiritual qualities you want to represent on your altar. The lists do not contain all the deities known to these ancient cultures.

Egypt

Amen/Amun/Ammon—God of reproduction, fertility, agriculture, prophecy. Associated with the ram and the goose.

Anubis—God of death, endings, wisdom, surgery, hospital stays, finding lost things, journeys, and protection. Considered a messenger from the gods to humans, he was associated with the jackal and sometimes the dog.

Bast—The cat-headed goddess of all animals, but especially cats. She symbolizes the moon, childbirth, fertility, pleasure, joy, music, dance, marriage, and healing.

Buto—Cobra goddess of protection.

Hathor—A mother and creatress goddess; protectress of women. Symbols include the moon, marriage, motherhood, artists, music, happiness, and prosperity. She is associated with the cow, the frog, and the cat.

Horus—God of the sun and the moon, he stands for prophecy, justice, success, and problem solving. Associated with the falcon and the hawk.

Imhotep—God of medicine and healing.

Isis—The supreme Egyptian goddess, who was honored for 3,000 years. In later times, her worship spread to Greece and Rome. Meanings include magic, fertility, marriage, purification, initiation, reincarnation, healing, divination, the arts, and protection. Associated with the cat, the goose, and the cow.

Maat—Goddess of judgment, truth, justice, and reincarnation. Associated with ostrich feathers.

Neith—A warrior-goddess and protectress, she represents magic, healing, mystical knowledge, domestic arts, and marriage. Two arrows were among her symbols. She was associated with the vulture.

Nephthys—The dark sister of Isis. Magic, protection, dreams, and intuition. The basket was one of her symbols.

Osiris—The supreme Egyptian god. Fertility, civilization, agriculture, crafts, judgment, architecture, social laws, power, growth, and stability. Associated with the hawk and the phoenix.

Ptah—God of artisans and artists, builders and craftsmen. Associated with the bull.

Sekhmet—The dark sister of Bast; a lion-headed goddess. Physicians and bonesetters; revenge, and power. Associated with the lioness.

Ta-Urt/Tauret—The hippopotamus goddess. Childbirth, maternity, and protection.

Thoth—God of books and learning, and the greatest of magicians. Writing, inventions, the arts, divination, commerce, healing, initiation, success, wisdom, truth, and the Akashic Records. Associated with the ibis.

Middle East

Addad—Canaan, Babylon, Assyria, Syria, Mesopotamia. God of storms, earthquakes, floods, and furious winds. Associated with lightning and the bull.

Adonis—Semitic god. Harvest, death, and resurrection. Associated with the boar.

Ahura Mazdah—Persia and Zoroastrianism. God of universal law, purification, and goodness. One of his symbols was the winged disk.

Asshur—Assyria, Babylon. Supreme god represented by a winged disk. Fertility, protection, victory, and bravery. Associated with the bull.

Astarte—Known as Ashtart in Phoenicia. Queen of Heaven. The moon, astrology, victory, revenge, and sexual love. Among her symbols were the eight-pointed star and the crescent.

Dumuzi/Tammuz—Mesopotamia, Sumeria. Called the Anointed God. Harvest and fertility.

Ea/Enki—Mesopotamia, Babylon, Sumeria. Creator god of carpenters, stonecutters, and goldsmiths; patron of all the arts. Associated with the goat, the fish, the eye, and the vase.

Enlil/Bel—Sumeria, Babylon, Assyria. King of the gods. Destructive winds, hurricanes, floods, storms, and the laws.

Inanna—Canaan, Phoenicia, Sumeria, Uruk, Babylon. Queen of the Heavens. Defense, victory, love, fertility, destiny, prosperity, and justice. Associated with the star, the serpent staff, and dogs.

Ishtar—Lady of Heaven. Patroness of priestesses; sexual love, fertility, revenge, resurrection, marriage, initiation, overcoming obstacles, and social laws. Associated with the lion, the serpent staff, the dragon, the eight-pointed star, the dove, the double ax, the rainbow, and the bridge. She had a rainbow necklace similar to that of the Norse goddess Freyja.

Lilith—Protectress of all pregnant women, mothers, and children. Associated with the owl.

Marduk—God of fate, courage, healing, justice, the law, and victory. Associated with the bull.

Mari/Meri/Marratu—Syria, Chaldea, Persia. Goddess of fertility, childbirth, the moon, and the sea. One of her symbols was the pearl.

Mithra/Mithras—Persia; god of many Middle Eastern cultures. The sun, warriors, contracts, predictions, wisdom, sacred oaths, prosperity, and spiritual illumination. Associated with the disk or circle and the cave.

Shamash/Chemosh—Mesopotamia, Sumeria, Babylon, Assyria. God of the sun, divination, retribution, courage, triumph, and justice.

Sin—Mesopotamia, Ur, Assyria, Babylon, Sumeria. God of the moon, the calendar, destiny, predictions, and secrets. Associated with lapis lazuli and the dragon.

Tiamat—Mesopotamia, Babylon, Sumeria. Goddess of destruction, karmic discipline, death, and regeneration. Associated with the dragon and the serpent.

Greece

Aphrodite—Goddess of love, sensuality, passion, partnerships, fertility, renewal, the sea, joy, and beauty. Associated with the swan, dove, poppy, rose, apple, and pomegranate.

Apollo—God of the light of the sun, healing, oracles, poetry, music, inspiration, magic, and the arts. Associated with the arrow, bay laurel, and the raven.

Ares—God of war, terror, courage, raw energy, and stamina.

Artemis—Virgin Huntress. Goddess of wild places and wild animals; protectress of young girls. Magic, psychic power, fertility, childbirth, sports, contact with nature, and mental healing. Associated with dogs, the stag, horse, acorn, crescent, and juniper.

Athena/Athene—Goddess of Athens. Freedom and women's rights; patroness of career women; patroness of craftsmen. Wisdom, justice, writing, music, the sciences, inventions, weaving, architects, and renewal. Associated with the owl, horse, intertwined snakes, the olive, and oak.

Cybele—A Phrygian Great Mother goddess of the earth and caverns; associated with the god Attis. Goddess of the natural world and wild beasts. The moon, magic, wildlife, and the dead. Originally worshipped in the form of a black meteorite, Cybele's worship spread to ancient Greece and Rome. Associated with the lion, bees, pomegranate, violets, pine, cypress, the cave, bowl, and pearl.

Demeter—Goddess of the Eleusinian Mysteries. Protectress of women; crops, initiation, renewal, fertility, civilization, the law, motherhood, and marriage. Associated with corn and wheat.

Dionysus—Known as the Twice-Born God. God of pleasure, the woodlands, wine, initiation, and rebirth. Associated with the vine, wine, ivy, the basket, and chalice.

Gaea/Gaia—Earth Goddess. Oaths, divination, healing, motherhood, marriage, and dreams. The Oracle at Delphi was originally hers, before Apollo took over. Associated with the laurel.

Hades—God of the Underworld. Elimination of fear of the dead. Associated with gemstones.

Hecate—A Thracian Triple Goddess of the moon and the Underworld with great power. Patroness of priestesses. The moon, prophecy, averting evil, riches, victory, travelers, crossroads, transformation, purification, and renewal. Associated with the snake, dragon, dogs, and cauldron.

Helios—God of the actual sun, riches, and enlightenment.

Hephaestus—God of blacksmiths, metalworkers, craftsmen, and volcanoes. Associated with pottery.

Hera—Queen of the Gods. Use her image when facing infidelity and insecurity, and also for marriage and childbirth. Associated with the peacock, cow, pomegranate, marjoram, lily, apple, flowers, willow, the sickle, and double ax.

Hermes—Messenger of the Gods. Commerce, good luck, orthodox medicine, occult wisdom, music, merchants, and diplomacy. Associated with the ram.

Hestia—Virgin Goddess of the hearth. The home, dedication to duty, and discipline. Her name was mentioned by the Greeks in all their prayers and sacrifices.

Nike—Goddess of victory. Associated with the palm branch.

Pan—God of male sexuality, animals, fertility, farming, medicine, and soothsaying. Associated with goats, fish, and bees.

Persephone—Queen of the Underworld. The seasons, crops, and overcoming obstacles. Associated with the bat, willow, narcissus, pomegranate, sheaf, corn, and cornucopia.

Poseidon—God of the seas and all sea animals. Storms, hurricanes, earthquakes, horses, rain, human emotions, sailors, and weather. Associated with the horse, fish, dolphin, and bull.

Themis—Goddess of law and order. Associated with the scales.

Zeus—God of the Heavens. Rain, storms, lightning, wisdom, justice, the law, riches, and the heart's desires. Associated with the eagle, oak, and lightning.

Rome

Bacchus/Liber—God of good times, wine, and fertility. Associated with the goat and vine.

Ceres—The Grain Goddess. Crops, initiation, protectress of women, and motherhood. Associated with corn and wheat.

Diana—Goddess of the woodlands and wild animals. Childbirth and women. Associated with deer, dogs, and the stag.

Faunus/Lupercus—God of nature and woodlands. Farming, music, dance, and agriculture. Associated with the goat, bees, and fish.

Fortuna—Goddess of fate, oracles, and chance. Associated with the wheel and cornucopia.

Janus—God of two faces representing the past and the future. Beginnings and endings, new cycles, and journeys. Associated with doors.

Juno—Queen of Heaven. Women's fertility, childbirth, the home, and marriage. Associated with the peacock, goose, and the veil.

Jupiter—King of Heaven. Storms, rain, honor, riches, friendships, the heart's desires, and protection. Associated with lightning.

Mars—God of war, terror, revenge, and courage. Associated with the woodpecker, horse, wolf, oak, and laurel.

Mercury—Messenger of the Gods. God of commerce, cunning, success, magic, travel, and merchants. Associated with the caduceus.

Minerva—Goddess of women's rights and freedom. Artisans, craftsmen, renewal, and protection. Associated with spinning and weaving, the owl, horse, snake, spear, and pillar.

Neptune—Sea god of earthquakes, storms, ships, the seas, and horses. Also associated with the bull and the dolphin.

Saturn—God of abundance, prosperity, and karmic lessons. Associated with the sickle, corn, and the vine.

Venus—Goddess of love, fertility, and renewal. Associated with the dove.

Africa

Ala/Ale—Nigeria. Earth Mother and creator goddess. Community laws, morality, and oaths.

Asa—Kenya. God of mercy; surviving the impossible or insurmountable.

Fa—Dahomey. God of personal destiny.

Famian—Guinea. God of fertility and protector against demons.

Katonda—East Africa. God of judgment, aid against all odds, and divination.

Mbaba Mwana Waresa—Zulu. Goddess of the rainbow and crops.

Mukuru—Southwest Africa. God of rain, healing, and protection.

Mungo—Kenya. God of rain.

Nyame—West Africa. God who prepared the soul for rebirth.

Ogun—West Africa. God of iron and warfare; removal of difficulties, and justice.

Olorun—Yoruba. God of truth, foreseeing, and victory against odds.

Ruhanga—Banyoro. God of fertility, children, harvest, health, and rebirth.

Shango—Nigeria. God of storm and war.

Wele—Bantu. God of rain, storms, creativity, and prosperity.

Yemoya—Yoruba. Goddess of women and children.

The Celts

Angus Mac Og—Ireland. God of love. Associated with birds.

Anu—Ireland. Goddess of fertility, prosperity, and health. Associated with cows.

Arianrhod—Wales. Goddess of beauty and reincarnation. Associated with the wheel.

Badb—Ireland. Goddess of wisdom, inspiration, and enlightenment. Associated with the cauldron, crow, and raven.

Bel—Ireland. God of the sun, healing, science, success, and prosperity.

Blodeuwedd—Wales. Goddess of wisdom, lunar mysteries, and initiation. Associated with flowers and the owl.

Bran—Wales. God of prophecy, the arts, leadership, music, and writing. Associated with the raven.

Branwen—Wales. Goddess of love and beauty. Associated with the cauldron.

Brigit/Brighid—Ireland. Goddess of all feminine arts and crafts. Healing, inspiration, learning, poetry, divination, and occult knowledge. Associated with weaving.

Cernunnos—Known to all Celtic areas. God of the woodlands and wild animals. Fertility, physical love, reincarnation, and wealth. Associated with the serpent, stag, ram, and bull.

Cerridwen—Wales. Goddess of regeneration, initiation, inspiration, magic, poetry, and knowledge. Associated with the cauldron and the sow.

The Dagda—Ireland. High King of the Tuatha De Danann, the ancient Irish deities. Patron of priests; the arts, prophecy, weather, reincarnation, knowledge, healing, and prosperity.

Danu—Ireland. Goddess of prosperity, magic, and wisdom.

Diancecht—Ireland. God of healing, medicine, and regeneration. Associated with herbs and the snake.

Epona—Britain, Gaul. Goddess of horses, dogs, and prosperity.

Lugh—Ireland, Wales. God of crafts, the arts, magic, journeys, healing, initiation, and prophecy. Associated with the raven, stag, and dog.

Macha—Ireland. Goddess of war, cunning, sexuality, and dominance over males. Associated with the raven and crow.

Manannan Mac Lir/Manawydan ap Llyr—Ireland, Wales. God of magic, storms, sailors, weather forecasting, merchants, and commerce. Associated with the pig, apple, and cauldron.

Morrigan—Ireland, Wales. Patroness of priestesses. Goddess of revenge, magic, and prophecy. Associated with the crow and raven.

Ogma—Ireland. God of poets and writers, physical strength, inspiration, and magic.

Scathach/Scota—Ireland, Scotland. Goddess of martial arts, blacksmiths, prophecy, and magic.

The Norse

Aegir—God of the sea, brewing, prosperity, sailors, and weather.

Audhumla—Goddess of motherhood, child-rearing, and home crafts. Associated with the cow.

Baldur/Balder—God of the sun, reconciliation, gentleness, reincarnation, and harmony.

Freyja/Freya—Mistress of cats and a shapeshifter. Goddess of love, sex, childbirth, enchantments, wealth, trance, wisdom, good luck, fertility, writing, and protection. Associated with the horse, cat, and amber.

Freyr/Frey—The god of Yule. God of fertility, love, abundance, horses, sailors, happiness, and weather. Associated with the boar.

Heimdall—God of the rainbow, beginnings and endings, and defense against evil. Associated with the bridge.

Hel—Queen of the Underworld. Revenge, fate, and karma.

Idunn/Idun—Goddess of immortality, youth, and long life. Associated with the apple.

Loki—A trickster and shapechanger. God of earthquakes, fire, cunning, deceit, daring, and revenge. Associated with the wolf and snake.

Njord—God of the sea, fishing, sailors, prosperity, and journeys.

Odin/Odhinn—King of the Gods. God of runes, poetry, magic, divination, storms, rebirth, knowledge, weather, justice, and inspiration. Associated with the wolf and raven.

Thor/Thorr—Protector of the common person. God of thunder, storms, law and order, strength, weather, and trading voyages. Associated with the goat, oak, and lightning.

Tyr—The bravest of the gods. God of victory, justice, the law, honor, and athletics.

Russia–Slavonia

Baba-Yaga—Goddess of endings, death, and revenge. Associated with the snake.

Dazhbog—God of the sun, fair judgment, and destiny.

Diiwica—Goddess of the hunt and the forests, hounds, victory, and success. Associated with the horse and dog.

Dzidzileyla/Didilia—Goddess of marriage, fertility, and love.

Mati Syra Zemlya—Goddess of the earth, crops, fertility, oaths, justice, divination, and property disputes.

Perun—God of storms, purification, fertility, oracles, defense against illness, victory, and oak forests. Associated with the cock, goat, bear, bull, and lightning.

Svantovit—Four-headed god of divination, prosperity, victory, and battles. Associated with the horse.

India

Agni—God of fire, rain, storms, protector of the home, new beginnings, and justice.

Brahma—God of creation and wisdom; often portrayed as having four heads, each facing a different direction. Associated with the swan.

Buddha—The Enlightened One, the Awakened One; the Way-Shower.

Chandra/Soma—Moon god of psychic visions and dreams.

Durga—Goddess of nurturing, protection, and defense. Associated with the lion and bowl.

Ganesha—Elephant-headed god of beginnings, writing, worldly success, learning, prosperity, journeys, and overcoming obstacles. Associated with the elephant and flowers.

Indra—King of the Gods. God of fertility, reincarnation, rain, the rainbow, the law, opposition to evil, creativity, and the sun. Associated with the elephant, horse, dog, and lightning.

Kali/Kali Ma—Goddess of Death. Goddess of regeneration, sexual love, and revenge; protectress of women. Associated with the wheel, knot, braid, and snake.

Krishna—God of erotic delights and music, and savior from sin. Associated with the star.

Lakshmi—Goddess of love, beauty, creative energy, agriculture, good fortune, prosperity, and success.

Sarasvati—Goddess of the creative arts, science, and teaching. Associated with the lotus and crescent.

Shiva—Demon-Slayer. He is shown with a third eye in the center of his forehead and four arms. God of fertility, physical love, medicine, storms, long life, healing, righteousness, and judgment. Associated with cattle, the bull, elephant, serpent, lightning, and the hourglass.

Tara—Goddess of spiritual enlightenment, knowledge, and compassion. In Tibet, Tara has twenty-one forms and colors, the most familiar forms being the Green Tara for growth and protection, and the White Tara for long life, health, and prosperity.

Vishnu—God of peace, power, compassion, abundance, and success. Associated with the lotus, serpent, and shells.

China

Chuang-Mu—Goddess of the bedroom and sexual delights.

Erh-Lang—God of protection from evil.

Fu-Hsi—God of happiness, destiny, and success. Associated with the bat.

Hsuan-T'ien-Shang-Ti—God of exorcism of evil spirits.

Kuan Yin—Goddess of fertility, children, motherhood, childbirth, and mercy. She is often portrayed holding a child in one arm and a willow twig or lotus blossom in her other hand. Associated with the willow.

K'uei-Hsing—God of tests and examinations; protector of travelers.

Lei-King—God who punished the guilty that human laws did not touch.

Lu-Hsing—God of salaries and employees. Associated with deer.

Shen Nung—God of medicine.

Shou-Hsing—God of longevity and old people. Associated with the peach.

T'ai-Yueh-Ta-Ti—God of fortune, payment of karmic debt, and prosperity.

Tsai Shen—God of wealth. Associated with the carp and cock.

Tsao-Wang—God of the hearth and kitchen. He is said to guard the hearth and family, allotting the next year's fortune.

Twen-Ch'ang—God of literature and poetry.

Yao-Shih—Master of healing and psychic abilities.

Japan

Amaterasu—Sun goddess of harvest, fertility, and light. Associated with weaving.

Benten—Goddess of good luck and protection from earthquakes.

Benzaiten—Goddess of love.

Bishamonten—God of happiness.

Daikoku—God of prosperity.

Ebisu—God of work.

Fukurokuju—God of happiness and long life.

Hotei Osho—God of good fortune.

Inari—Fox-goddess of merchants, business, and prosperity. Associated with the fox and rice.

Jizo Bosatsu—Protector of women in childbirth, and children.

Jurojin—God of happiness and long life.

Kishi-Mojin—Goddess of children, compassion, and fertility.

Native North America

Agloolik—Eskimo. God of hunters and fishermen.

Ataentsic—Iroquois/Huron. Goddess of marriage and childbirth.

Ioskeha—Iroquois/Huron. God who defeats demons and heals diseases.

Onatha—Iroquois. Goddess of wheat and harvest.

Spider Woman—Navajo. Goddess of charms and magic.

Tirawa—Pawnee. God of hunting, agriculture, and religious rituals.

Wakonda—Lakota. God of all wisdom and power.

Yanauluha—Zuni. The great medicine god. Civilization, animal husbandry, healing, and knowledge.

Mayas

Hurukan—God of fire, the whirlwind, hurricanes, and spiritual illumination.

Itzamna—God of knowledge, writing, fertility, regeneration, and medicine. Associated with the lizard.

Ixchel—Goddess of childbirth, medicine, pregnancy, and domestic arts, especially weaving.

Kukulcan—God of learning, culture, the laws, and the calendar.

Yum Caax—God of maize, fertility, riches, and life.

Aztecs

Chalchihuitlicuetlicue—Goddess of storms, whirlpools, love, and flowers.

Chantico—Goddess of the home, fertility, and wealth. Associated with snakes and gemstones.

Coatlicue—Goddess of famines and earthquakes. Associated with snakes.

Itzcoliuhqui—God of darkness, volcanic eruptions, and disaster. Associated with obsidian.

Itzpaplotl—Goddess of fate and agriculture.

Mayauel—Goddess of childbirth. Associated with the bowl, turtle, and snake.

Quetzalcoatl—God of wind, life breath, civilization, the arts, and fate.

Tlaloc—God of thunder, rain, fertility, and water. Associated with lightning and the pitcher or vase.

Tozi—Goddess of midwives, healers, and healing.

Incas

Chasca—Goddess of girls and flowers.

Inti—Sun god of fertility and crops. Associated with corn.

Mama Quilla—Goddess of married women and the calendar.

Pachacamac—God of the arts and occupations, and oracles.

Viracocha—God of the arts, the sun, storms, oracles, moral codes, and rain.

ANGELS AND ARCHANGELS

Angels have been known around the world and in many cultures outside of or prior to Christian influence, or before Christianity ever was formed. They have been called by many names, but their descriptions are remarkably similar. They are always described as messengers from the spirit world, helpers, and guardians of those who recognize and call upon them.

Camael—Visions, discretion, courage, exorcism, purification, and protection.

Gabriel—Resurrection, mercy, truth, hope, visions, divination, and herbal medicine.

Haniel—Love, beauty, and creativity; protection against evil.

Metatron—Spiritual enlightenment and mystical knowledge.

Michael—Truth, knowledge, divination, protection, repentance, deliverance from enemies, victory in battle, and protection from police harassment. Patron of police officers, paratroopers, and mariners.

Personal Guardian Angel—Protection, guidance in all things, and help with spiritual wisdom.

Raphael—Healing, harmony, success, honor, contacting your guardian angel, safe journeys, reuniting with loved ones, and curing all disease.

Ratziel—Illumination, guidance, and destiny.

Sandalphon—Seeing the guardian angel; stability, guidance, and protection.

Tzadquiel—Spiritual love and good fortune.

Tzaphkiel—Spiritual development, overcoming grief, and balancing or changing karma.

Uriel—Teaching, insight, stability, and endurance.

SAINTS

Certain Christian saints are called upon for specific help. This usually takes the form of prayers and an offering of a candle when the petition is made. The Vatican Council of the Catholic Church addressed this devotion to the saints in their Constitution on the Church, No. 50, saying that the saints were helpful friends in heaven. These devotions usually consist of saying prayers, lighting candles, and offering flowers or incense.

The Infant Jesus of Prague—Health matters, surgery, guidance, and wisdom.

Our Lady of Fatima—Protection from evil and the anger of adversaries, and freedom from any situation that restricts and binds.

Our Lady of Guadelupe—Peace, sickness, luck, and help in any situation.

Our Lady of the Immaculate Conception—Sickness and fertility.

Our Lady of Loretto—Help when looking for a place to live, protection when traveling by air, and peace in the family. Patroness of pilots and home builders.

Our Lady of Lourdes—Sickness and regaining health.

Our Lady of Mercy—Peace, health, justice, and release from jail.

Our Lady of Mount Carmel—Protection from accidents or sudden death.

St. Agabus—Patron of psychics and clairvoyant visions.

St. Agatha—Breast diseases, rape, and volcanic eruptions. Patroness of nurses.

St. Agnes—Fidelity, finding a suitable mate, and relationships.

St. Agricola of Avignon—Protection against misfortune, bad luck, and plagues. Patron of rain.

St. Albinus—Gallstones and kidney disease.

St. Alexis—Keeping enemies away.

St. Alphonsus Liguori—Rheumatic fever, arthritis, gout, joint and muscle ailments, osteoarthritis.

Sts. Alodia and Nunilo—Patronesses of child abuse victims and runaways.

St. Aloysius—Fever, epidemics, plagues, and settling disputes.

St. Andrew—Patron of fishermen.

St. Ann—Help with deafness and blindness, and with special requests. Patroness of women, particularly those in childbirth.

St. Anthony—Finding lost items, marriage or love problems, financial problems, and getting a job. Considered a wonderworker.

St. Apollonia—Patron of toothaches and dentists.

St. Arthelius—Patroness of kidnapping victims.

St. Barbara—Protectress of women; love, help against those trying to break up a marriage, clearing a path through obstacles, release from prison, and driving away evil. Patroness of prisoners, architects, the military, prisoners, and stoneworkers.

St. Bartholomew—Learning the truth, protection from violence, and surgery. Patron of surgeons.

St. Benedict—Fever, kidney disease, poisons, contagious diseases, safe delivery in childbirth, sick animals, business success, and protection from storms.

St. Bernardine of Siena—Gambling addictions.

St. Blaise—Diseases in both humans and animals, especially throat diseases. Patron of veterinarians.

St. Brigid of Kildare—Childbirth, fertility, protection from fires, healing, agriculture, inspiration, learning, poetry, prophecy, and love. Patroness of blacksmiths, dairy workers, and physicians.

St. Cadoc of Wales—Glandular disorders.

St. Capistrano—Repelling enemies.

St. Clare of Assisi—Understanding, help with difficulties, and overcoming drug and alcohol problems.

St. Catherine of Alexandria—Beauty, fertility, a peaceful death, love, jealousy, healing, fortunate birth, visions and dreams, and public speaking. Patroness of teachers and jurors.

St. Catherine of Siena—Patroness of nursing homes, fire protection, and unmarried women.

St. Cecilia—Success in composing; music, poets, and singers.

St. Christopher—Protection from accidents and sudden death; safe travel, fevers, storms, and nightmares. Patroness of unmarried men, bus drivers, and motorists.

St. Cipriano—Protection while traveling; homeless people, earthquakes, fire, bad neighbors, liars, deceitful lovers, and keeping one out of jail.

St. Clotilde—Adopted children and widows.

Sts. Cosmas and Damian—Sickness, correct diagnosis of diseases, and removal of obstacles. Patrons of barbers, druggists, physicians, and surgeons.

St. Denis—Headaches.

St. Dismas—Patron of prisoners, thieves, death-row inmates, and undertakers.

St. Dorothy of Montau—Miscarriages.

St. Dymphna—Insanity, nervous disorders or any mental problems, family harmony, and epilepsy.

St. Elmo—Appendicitis, intestinal disease, and seasickness.

St. Expedite—Settling disputes and changing things quickly.

St. Fabiola—Infidelity and physical abuse. Patroness of divorce and widows.

St. Florian—Protection of the home against fire and flood; help in danger and emergencies. Patron of firemen.

St. Francis de Sales—Deafness. Patron of writers and journalists.

St. Francis of Assisi—Understanding, peace, spiritual wisdom, and help with problems. Patron of all animals and birds, gardens, firemen, merchants, and garment makers.

St. Francis Xavier Cabrini—The poor; being accepted when you move; health, and education. Patroness of emigrants.

St. George—Courage, conquering fear, overcoming jealousy; skin diseases, and mental retardation. Patron of soldiers.

St. Gerard Majella—Fertility, pregnant women, mothers with small children, being falsely accused, channeling, prophecy, healing, and seeing the truth. Patron of pregnant women.

St. Gertrude of Nivelles—Getting rid of rats and mice. Patron of cats.

St. Giles—Patron of the physically disabled.

St. Helen of Jerusalem—Love and overcoming sorrow. Patroness of archaeologists.

St. Hippolytus—Patron of horses.

St. Hubert—Patron of dogs, hunters, and rabies sufferers.

St. Ignatius of Loyola—Protection against burglars and evil spirits. Patron of soldiers.

St. James the Greater—Conquering enemies, removing obstacles; justice, arthritis, and rheumatism. Patron of manual laborers.

St. Joan of Arc—Courage, spiritual strength, and overcoming enemies.

St. John the Baptist—Good luck, crops, and protection from enemies. Patron of tailors.

St. John Bosco—Temporal needs, students, and trouble with children. Patron of editors.

St. John Gualbert—Patron of foresters and park services.

St. John the Divine—Friendship. Patron of art dealers, editors, and publishers.

St. Joseph—Protection, finding a job, selling a house; married couples. Patron of carpenters and bakers.

St. Jude—Hopeless cases, court troubles or getting out of jail; drugs.

St. Lawrence—A peaceful home and family, and financial assistance. Patron of the poor.

St. Lazarus—Sickness, diseases of the legs, drug addiction, and getting prosperity.

St. Leonard—Burglary, prisoners of war, and women in labor.

St. Louis Bertrand—Learning languages, and protection from evil and accidents.

St. Lucy—Eye problems, repelling legal problems, settling court cases, protection from hexes; help when your back is against the wall. Patroness of salespeople and writers.

St. Luke—Patron of painters, physicians, and surgeons.

St. Madron—Pain.

St. Martha—Domestic problems, money troubles, keeping a lover or husband faithful, bringing in a new love, and conquering enemies. Patroness of housekeepers and servants.

St. Martin de Porres—Financial needs, health, and harmony. Patron of the poor and animals.

St. Martin of Tours—Repelling evil, protection from enemies; money, luck, and a successful business.

St. Mary Magdalene—Patroness of repentant prostitutes, perfumers, and hair stylists.

St. Matthew—Patron of bankers, bookkeepers, customs agents, security guards, and tax collectors.

St. Michael—Total protection.

St. Nicholas of Myra—Patron of dock workers, children, brides, merchants, unmarried women, and travelers.

St. Patrick—Prosperity, good luck, spiritual wisdom, guidance, and protection against snakebite.

St. Paul—Courage, overcoming opposition, and a peaceful home. Patron of authors, journalists, publishers, and travelers.

St. Peregrine Laziosi—Health problems, particularly cancer.

St. Peter—Success, good business, strength, courage, good luck, and removing obstacles. Patron of bridge builders and masons.

St. Philomena—Pregnant women, destitute mothers, fertility, trouble with children, happiness in the home, money problems, mental illness, and real estate. Patroness of any desperate situation.

St. Raymond Nonnatus—Stopping gossip and protection of unborn babies. Patron of midwives.

St. Rita—Bleeding, desperate situations, parenthood, infertility, and marital problems.

St. Rita of Cascia—Loneliness, abusive relationships, healing wounds and tumors, and deliverance from evil. Patroness of hopeless cases.

St. Sebastian—Justice, court cases, overcoming rivals, removing obstacles, and obtaining good fortune. Patron of athletes, gardeners, potters, stonemasons, and soldiers.

St. Teresa of Avila—Headaches and heart attacks.

St. Therese of Lisieux—Alcohol and drug problems, spiritual growth, protection against black magic, and tuberculosis.

St. Thomas Aquinas—Improving the memory and passing school exams. Patron of scholars and students.

St. Vitus—Exorcism of evil spirits and curing epilepsy. Patron of comedians and dancers.

Virgin Mary—The mother of the Christ. Love, kindness, protection, and intercession for any need.

CHAPTER 4

Building Special Altars

The object of any altar is for it to symbolize what you want to attract into your life. Your altar should be pleasing to you, not necessarily to anyone else. To make your altar more powerful, concentrate on your objective while arranging the objects on it, then visit the altar frequently. The following examples are only suggestions to give you ideas for your own creations. You may change any or all of the objects and symbols. See Chapter 3 for more information on the meaning of objects and symbols.

An altar need not be anything fancy. It can be a small table, a shelf in the kitchen or bathroom, or some other available space. In fact, you may decide to prepare different altars for different rooms. If you use candles on your altars, be certain that they can burn without creating a fire hazard. Do not burn candles under another shelf, near curtains or hanging fabrics, and always put candles in a nonflammable, unbreakable holder.

The deities listed do not include all the appropriate deities or saints who can help with the problem for which you are building your altar. You may not wish to include any deity statue, or you may wish to have several. The choice is yours.

There is no one proper place on an altar to place any object. Work with arrangements until the altar is pleasing to your eye and your soul. Candles may be used on any altar, as may incense. Consult the list of colors in Chapter 3 to choose an appropriately colored candle. If you wish, anoint it with a corresponding oil before burning it. You may have as many candles as you wish on an altar, either all of the same color, or a combination of several appropriate colors. The color white can be added safely and effectively to any altar arrangement. Never leave wilted flowers on an altar; replace them whenever necessary.

An altar may be left unchanged for a long period, or rearranged and changed whenever you feel it is necessary. An altar is a very personal, individual expression and should not reflect the desires of another person.

LOVE

When building an altar to attract love into your life, you should never specify a particular person. This not only limits your choices, but may well bring about a relationship that is not the one you expected. Also, you do not want to create negative karma by trying to make an uninterested person love you. You most definitely should not try to separate a couple.

Examples of altar objects: Statues or pictures of a cat or dove; symbol of a basket or heart; the colors pink and green; the stones rose quartz, garnet, and lapis lazuli; the herb ginger; the tree mistletoe; the oil and incense violet; the flower red carnation.

Examples of deities: Aphrodite, Inanna, Haniel, St. Martha.

Suggested arrangement: Place the cat statue next to a small basket with a red heart inside. The colors may be used in an altar cloth and/or the candles. You may wish to write out on a piece of paper the characteristics you value in a love relationship; then put the paper into the basket with the heart. Sprinkle ginger lightly over the items in the basket, or place a piece of mistletoe in with the heart. Arrange the stones near the statue, with the incense nearby. Use a small vase for the red carnation.

PROSPERITY

Your first prosperity altar may be for short-term financial relief. However, you also need to concentrate on long-term prosperity. To achieve this, you need to work for good opportunities to come your way, ones that will help you achieve what you desire. Nothing comes free, so do not expect to win a huge lottery.

Examples of altar objects: Statues or pictures of a pig or dragon; symbols of a box and a cauldron; the colors brown, green, or gold; the stones turquoise, moss agate, or tiger's eye; the tree fig; the herb ginger; the oil and incense patchouli; the flower hollyhock or jasmine.

Examples of deities: Fortuna, Freyr, Raphael, St. Anthony.

Suggested arrangement: Place the cauldron in the center of your altar space and place inside it the stones and a little of the herb. The box can hold a list of the reasons you want to increase your prosperity. By making this list, you convince your subconscious mind that you have a need and the right to ask for the opportunities to increase your wealth. The colors may be used in altar cloths and/or candles. Hollyhock blossoms can be floated in a shallow bowl and jasmine placed in an elegant vase.

PROTECTION

Protection altars can be built for protection from specific dangers or simply to protect against negative thoughts coming from jealous or hateful people. If your altar is for protection from a specific threatening person, such as an ex-spouse, ex-lover, or harmful family member, try to place a photo of the offending person under the deity or animal statue that symbolizes divine wisdom and the power to overcome the threat.

Examples of altar objects: Statues or pictures of a tiger or wolf; keys; symbols of a ring or circle; the colors black and indigo; the stones amber, carnelian, and black obsidian; the tree holly; the herb basil or bay; the oil and incense lavender; the flower peony.

Examples of deities: Heimdall, Thor, Guardian Angel, St. Michael, St. Christopher.

Suggested arrangement: Place the statue in the center of the altar so that the animal figure has a prominent place. Around it, position the stones, keys, and either a ring or a drawing of a circle. Holly twigs and the herb may be placed at both ends to produce protective energies. Place the incense, candles, and flower to make an eye-pleasing arrangement.

THANKSGIVING

Thanksgiving altars can be built for a number of reasons: recovery from an illness, finding a wonderful friend or lover, success in obtaining a good job or home, escape from a potential danger, and so on.

Examples of altar objects: Statues or pictures of a unicorn or blackbird; symbols of a shell or the yin/yang symbol; the color white; the stones clear quartz crystal and chrysoprase; the tree cedar; the herb, oil, and incense myrrh; the flower a white rose.

Examples of deities: Buddha, Bishamonten, Metatron, the Virgin Mary.

Suggested arrangement: Choose a nice vase for the rose and set it in the center of the altar. Around it, arrange the stones, symbols, and animal statue. To represent the tree, you may have any object made of cedar, or else burn cedar incense. If you use a cedar box or bowl, you may want to write out on a small piece of paper why you are thankful, and place that inside the cedar container.

SPIRITUAL GROWTH

Altars for spiritual growth are not that common, as most people are usually more intent on improving their lives in other areas. However, there will come a time when only spiritual growth on your part will improve your life and bring it into balance.

Examples of altar objects: Statues or pictures of a goose or raven; a symbol representing a bridge or wings; the colors magenta or purple; the stones amethyst and clear quartz crystal; the tree pine or another evergreen; the herb hyssop or mugwort; the oil and incense lotus; the flower lily.

Examples of deities: Tara, Isis, Metatron, St. Francis of Assisi.

Suggested arrangement: Either place a picture of the bridge or wings to the rear center of the altar or fasten it to the wall directly behind the altar. In front of the picture, place the animal statue and the stones, with the pine or evergreens arranged around them. The herb may be tucked in among the pine boughs, and the lily can be floated in a shallow bowl next to the candles and incense.

This altar is excellent for meditation on self-discovery and your personal life path.

FINDING A JOB

Although you must be sincere in your efforts and desires to obtain a good job, you do not have to be absolutely specific in every detail. You want to create opportunities for yourself. Once the opportunities present themselves, it is up to you to make the effort of applying for the job and doing your best once you get it.

Examples of altar objects: Statues or pictures of a bat, coyote, or frog; symbols of breasts, a box, or cube; the colors black and orange; the stones bloodstone and malachite; the tree bay; the herb thyme; the oil and incense ginger; the flower aster or ivy.

Examples of deities: Ganesha, Ebisu, Ptah, Sandalphon, St. Joseph.

Suggested arrangement: Write out the type of job you wish on a small piece of paper. Place the paper either in the center of your altar or inside a box there. Set the stones on top of the paper or box. Twine the ivy around the box, or place the asters nearby in a vase. Sprinkle a little thyme and bay leaves over the altar. Place the black candle (for absorbing negativity) on one side of the altar and the orange (for action and increasing the intellect) on the other. Place the animal statue near the paper or box, to watch over it.

MAKING A DECISION

Sometimes you feel you cannot make a decision because you feel inadequate or do not have all the facts. A decision-making altar will help bring the information and courage you need if you meditate before it once a day.

Examples of altar objects: Statues or pictures of an elephant, eagle, or bee; symbols of an ear of corn or an eye; the colors gold, red, and yellow; the stones fluorite and pyrite; the tree apple; the herb sage or catnip; the incense clove; the flower aster or chrysanthemum.

Examples of deities: Horus, Ganesha, Ratziel, St. Sebastian.

In the Far East, the elephant with an upraised trunk symbolizes good fortune; in India, the elephant-god Ganesha is said to remove obstacles. Therefore, an elephant of any kind is symbolic of moving ahead in life by making the right decisions.

Suggested arrangement: Surround your animal statue with the stones, and place the vase of flowers nearby. An apple can represent the apple tree. Place it together with the ear of corn to symbolize abundance. Sprinkle the herbs before the animal statue, and use the colors in candles.

RECOVERING FROM DIVORCE

Most divorces do not end amicably. They tend to sour with bitterness, recrimination, and sometimes threats by one or both parties. The parties involved forget the old saying: The best revenge is to live a good life. You need to move beyond all these negatives and let go of the past in order to accept the future. Never put a photo of the divorced partner on your altar, only your own photo. This altar is for *your* healing from the divorce. Choose a photo where you are smiling and happy, a symbol of what you will have in your future.

Examples of altar objects: Statues or pictures of a badger or bear; symbols of a mask, knots, door, scepter (wand), or square; the colors red or black; the stones brown or orange and brown agate, amber, or chrysoprase; the tree holly or juniper; the oil and incense patchouli, the herb mint; the flower anemone or chrysanthemum.

Examples of deities: Anubis, Buto, Uriel, St. Fabiola.

Suggested arrangement: Place your smiling photo in the center of the altar, representing your central importance in your new life. Put the animal statue, symbols, stones, and herbs in a semicircle before it. These items will be a daily reminder that you are guided and protected as you forge a new existence for yourself. Arrange the bouquet of flowers on one end of the altar, the candles and incense on the other, for balance.

HEALING

This altar may be for you, another person, or a pet in need of healing. In fact, you can arrange groups of photos of friends and family who need divine healing energies. This altar may be an ongoing, changeable altar that becomes a source of hope and inspiration to many.

Examples of altar objects: Statues or pictures of a dog or phoenix; symbols of the caduceus, arrows, ring, jar, or yin/yang; colors light blue and green; stones of hematite and clear quartz crystal; the tree holly or oak; the herb rue; the oil and incense pine; the flower bachelor's button or lilac.

Examples of deities: Brigit, Yao-Shih, Imhotep, Raphael, Sts. Cosmas and Damian.

Suggested arrangement: If you have only one photo of someone needing healing, place it in the center of the altar. If you have several photos, arrange them in a line across the altar so you can clearly see each one. Place the animal statue, stones, herb, incense, candles, flowers, and symbols around or among these photos. This will keep the flow of healing energy moving among the sick people at all times.

IN MEMORY OF LOST LOVED ONES

Some people already have "altars" to lost loved ones, although they may be unaware of this. Pictures of deceased friends and family may cover the top of the piano or a table in the living room. This is an excellent way to remember loved ones, as well as to remind others of their continued existence in our hearts and in another realm.

If you are having difficulty coming to terms with the loss of someone, whether recent or not, a special altar holding shared objects, photos, and other mementos can help. When you feel the hurt has been healed, you can move the photos to stand among others of beloved family and friends, living and deceased.

Examples of altar objects: Statues or pictures of a deer, hawk, or raven; symbol of a star, peach, or pumpkin; the colors white and royal blue; the stones bloodstone and black onyx; the herb rosemary; the tree yew or pomegranate; the oil and incense lily; flowers rose and periwinkle.

Examples of deities: Osiris, Ishtar, Tzaphkiel, the Virgin Mary.

Arrange this altar in whatever way seems best to you. This

is a symbol of your personal grief over the loss of someone dear to you. Add or remove personal mementos as time passes and your degree of grief changes. There will come a time when the deep hurt lessens, and you will not be grieving before this altar so much. The pain never completely goes away, but you will learn how to handle it better.

DEDICATION TO GOD/GODDESS/SAINT

Some people find they can move through life with more ease if they have one special altar dedicated to a deity or saint of their choice. This altar is one that you should visit daily for help with your everyday life. Commune with the deity or saint through meditation and prayer.

Examples of altar objects: Statues or pictures of your chosen deity or saint; the colors white, gold, and silver; the stones clear quartz crystal, black obsidian, amethyst, lapis lazuli, malachite, and rose quartz; the flowers sunflower or red and white roses; the oil and incense rose.

Place the deity or saint statue in the center of the altar as the prominent object. Arrange the stones, candles, and flowers about this statue in whatever way seems best to you. Requests written on paper can also be placed on the altar.

Resources

The following businesses sell a variety of products and ritual supplies. Although some catalogs are free, it is best to contact a business to ask about a catalog and its possible price.

All One Tribe Drums
P.O. Drawer N, Taos, NM 87571. Handmade drums with Native American designs.

Altar Egos Gallery
110 West Houston Street, New York, NY 10012. Statues, candles, cloths, bowls, cauldrons, chalices.

Aphrodesia
264 Bleecker Street, New York, NY 10014. All varieties of herbs.

Azure Green
P.O. Box 48, Middlefield, MA 01243-0048. E-mail: AbyssDist@aol.com. Web site: www.Azuregreen.com. Candles, incense, stones, statues, and many other items.

Barbara Steele
P.O. Box 2424, Guerneville, CA 95446-2424. Custom hand-crafted cedar altars.

Crescent Moongoddess
P.O. Box 153, Massapequa Park, NY 11762. E-mail: cres-moon@crescentmoongoddess.com. Web site: www.crescent-moongoddess.com. Handmade wands, chalices, altar patents, incense burners, cauldrons, candles, oils, incense.

Earth Star Connection
1218 31st Street, N.W., Washington, D.C. 20007. Candles, incense, drums, rattles, crystals, and minerals.

Feng Shui Warehouse
P.O. Box 6689, San Diego, CA 92166. Books and supplies for practicing feng shui placement.

Gifts of the Spirit
P.O. Box 772, Belle Meade, NJ 08502. Altar cloths, candles, incense, rosaries.

The Great Goddess Collection, Star River Productions, Inc.
P.O. Box 510642, Melbourne Beach, FL 32951. Goddess images.

The Hero's Journey
2440 Broadway, New York, NY 10024. Drums, rattles, and more.

Home of the Buddhas
1223 Summerwind Way, Milpitas, CA 95035. Statues of Buddha, Ganesha, Tara, and others.

Mystic Trader
1334 Pacific Avenue, Forest Grove, OR 97116. Statuary, incense, smudge sticks, musical instruments, and many Eastern items.

The Nature Company
P.O. Box 188, Florence, KY 41022. Gemstones, minerals.

Pyramid Collection, Altid Park
P.O. Box 3333, Chelmsford, MA 01824-0933. Wide range of items, including crystals, stones, musical instruments, and statues.

The Red Rose Collection
826 Burlway, Burlingame, CA 94010. Bowls, smudge pots, and more.

Sacred Source (JBL Statues)
P.O. Box 163, Crozet, VA 22932. E-mail: spirit@sacred-source.com. $2.00 catalog. A wide range of deity statues from many cultures.

Shasta Abbey Buddhist Supplies
P.O. Box 199, Mt. Shasta, CA 96067. Altar shelves, cabinets, statues, incense, gongs, and more.

Sidedoor Press
2934 Lomita Road, Santa Barbara, CA 93105. Unfinished niche altars.

Three Jewels Design
P.O. Box 151116, San Rafael, CA 94915. Home and travel altars.

Bibliography

Altheim, Franz (1938). *A History of Roman Religion*, translated by Harold Mattingly. NY: no publisher.

Angus, S. (1975). *The Mystery-Religions.* NY: Dover Publications.

Bachofen, J. J. (1973). *Myth, Religion and Mother Right*, translated by Ralph Mannheim; ed. by Joseph Campbell. Princeton, NJ: Princeton UniversityPress.

Barber, Elizabeth Wayland (1994). *Women's Work: The First 20,000 Years.* NY: W. W. Norton & Co.

Baring, Anne, and Jules Cashford (1991). *The Myth of the Goddess: Evolution of an Image.* UK: Viking Arkana.

Beck, Renee, and Sydney Barbara Metrick (1990). *The Art of Ritual.* Berkeley, CA: Celestial Arts.

Bennett, Florence Mary (1987). (Originally published 1912.) *Religious Cults Associated with the Amazons.* NY: University Books.

Boulding, Elise (1978). *The Underside of History.* Boulder, CO: Westview Press.

Briffault, Robert (1952). *The Mothers: A Study of the Origins of Sentiments and Institutions.* 3 vols. NY: Macmillan.

Budge, E. A. Wallis (1978). *Amulets & Superstitions.* NY: Dover Publications.

———— (1969). *The Gods of the Egyptians.* 2 vols. NY: Dover Publications.

Campbell, Joseph (1968). *The Masks of God: Primitive Mythology*. NY: Penguin Books.

_____ (1974). *The Mythic Image*. Princeton, NJ: Princeton University Press.

_____ (1983). *The Way of the Animal Powers*. San Francisco, CA: Harper & Row.

Cavendish, Richard, ed. (1980). *Mythology: An Illustrated Encyclopedia*. NY: Rizzoli.

Cirlot, J. E. (1971). *A Dictionary of Symbols*, translated by Jack Sage. NY: Philosophical Library.

Conway, D. J. (1997). *Animal Magick*. St. Paul, MN: Llewellyn Publications.

_____ (1995). *By Oak, Ash and Thorn: Modern Celtic Shamanism*. St. Paul, MN: Llewellyn Publications.

_____ (1990). *Celtic Magic*. St. Paul, MN: Llewellyn Publications.

_____ (1999). *Crystal Enchantments: A Complete Guide to Stones and Their Magical Properties*. Freedom, CA: The Crossing Press.

_____ (1993). *Magick of the Gods and Goddesses*. St. Paul, MN: Llewellyn Publications, Originally titled *The Ancient & Shining Ones*.

_____ (1996). *Magickal, Mythical, Mystical Beasts*. St. Paul, MN: Llewellyn Publications.

_____ (1994). *Maiden, Mother, Crone*. St. Paul, MN: Llewellyn Publications.

Cotterell, Arthur, ed. (1989). *Macmillan Illustrated Encyclopedia of Myths and Legends*. NY: Macmillan.

D'Alviella, Count Goblet (1979). *Migration of Symbols*. UK: Aquarian Press.

Davidson, H. R. Ellis (1988). *Myths and Symbols in Pagan Europe.* Syracuse, NY: University Press.

Diner, Helen (1973). *Mothers and Amazons: The First Feminine History of Culture,* translated and ed. by John Philip Lunden. NY: Doubleday/Anchor.

Frazer, James G. (1963). *The Golden Bough.* NY: Macmillan.

Gimbutas, Marija (1991). *The Civilization of the Goddess.* San Francisco, CA: HarperSanFrancisco.

_____ (1982). *The Goddesses and Gods of Old Europe: Myths and Cult Images.* Berkeley, CA: University of California Press.

_____ (1989). *The Language of the Goddess.* San Francisco, CA: Harper & Row.

Graves, Robert (1978). *The White Goddess.* NY: Farrar, Straus & Giroux.

Gray, Louis Herbert, ed. (1916). *The Mythology of All Races.* Boston, MA.

Greenaway, Kate (1992. Originally published c. 1866). *Language of Flowers.* NY: Dover.

Guirand, Felix, ed. (1978). *New Larousse Encyclopedia of Mythology,* translated by Richard Aldington and Delano Ames. UK: Hamlyn.

Hooke, S. H. (1953). *Babylonian and Assyrian Religion.* UK: Hutchinson.

James, E. O. (1965). *From Cave to Cathedral: Temples and Shrines of Prehistoric, Classical, and Early Christian Times.* NY: Frederick A. Praeger.

_____ (1994). *The Cult of the Mother Goddess.* NY: Barnes & Noble Books.

Jobes, Gertrude (1962). *Dictionary of Mythology, Folklore and Symbols.* NY: Scarecrow Press.

Johnson, Buffie (1988). *Lady of the Beasts: Ancient Images of the Goddess and Her Sacred Animals.* San Francisco, CA: Harper & Row.

Jung, Carl G. (1990). *The Archetypes and the Collective Unconscious.* Princeton, NJ: Princeton University Press.

Kingston, Karen (1997). *Creating Sacred Space with Feng Shui.* NY: Broadway Books.

Kramer, Samuel N. (1963). *The Sumerians: Their History, Culture, and Character.* Chicago, IL: University of Chicago Press.

Larrington, Carolyne, ed. (1992). *The Feminist Companion to Mythology.* UK: Pandora Press.

Linn, Denise (1995). *Sacred Space: Clearing and Enhancing the Energy of Your Home.* NY: Ballantine Books.

Malbrough, Ray T. (1998). *The Magical Power of the Saints.* St. Paul, MN: Llewellyn Publications.

Nahmad, Claire (1998). *Garden Spells.* UK: Gramercy.

Neumann, Erich (1974). *The Great Mother: An Analysis of the Archetype,* translated by Ralph Mannheim. Princeton, NJ: Princeton University Press.

Rossbach, Sarah (1983). *Feng Shui: The Chinese Art of Placement.* NY: E. P. Dutton.

Sandoval, Annette (1997). *The Directory of Saints.* NY: Signet/Penguin.

Scobie, Grechen and Ann Field (1998). *The Meaning of Flowers.* San Francisco, CA: Chronicle Books.

Scully, Vincent (1979). *The Earth, the Temple, and the Gods.* New Haven, CT: Yale University Press.

Seaton, Beverly (1995). *Language of Flowers: A History.* Charlottesville, NC: University Press of Virginia.

Sjoo, Monica and Barbara Mor (1987). *The Great Cosmic Mother: Rediscovering the Religion of the Earth.* San Francisco, CA: Harper & Row.

Stone, Merlin (1990). *Ancient Mirrors of Womanhood: A Treasury of Goddess and Heroine Lore from Around the World.* Boston, MA: Beacon Press.

Streep, Peg (1997). *Altars Made Easy.* San Francisco, CA: HarperSanFrancisco.

Turville-Petre, E. O. G. (1964). *Myth and Religion of the North.* NY: Holt, Rinehart & Winston.

Vermaseren, Maarten J. (1977). *Cybele & Attis: The Myth & the Cult,* translated by A. M. H. Lemmers. UK: Thames & Hudson.

Ward, Marina (1985). *Alone of All Her Sex: The Myth and Cult of the Virgin Mary.* UK: Pan Books.

Warne, Frederick (1996). *Flower Fairies: The Meaning of Flowers.* UK: Penguin.

Wells, Diana (1997). *100 Flowers and How They Got Their Names.* Chapel Hill, NC: Algonquin Books of Chapel Hill.

Willetts, R. F. (1962). *Cretan Cults and Festivals.* UK: Routledge & Kegan Paul.

BOOKS BY THE CROSSING PRESS

A Little Book of Love Magic

By Patricia Telesco

A cornucopia of lore, magic, and imaginative ritual designed to bring excitement and romance to your life. Patricia Telesco tells us how to use magic to manifest our hopes and dreams for romantic relationships, friendships, family relations, and passions for our work.

$9.95 • Paper • ISBN 0-89594-887-7

A Little Book of Candle Magic

By D.J. Conway

D. J. Conway gives a thorough introduction to tapping the reservoirs of magic in candles. She provides chants, meditations, and affirmations to find a mate, achieve enlightenment, or improve life materially and spiritually, and she encourages readers to create their own.

$9.95 • Paper • ISBN 1-58091-043-2

Advanced Celtic Shamanism

By D. J. Conway

In her new book, Conway uses the four paths of shamanism (healer, bard, warrior, and mystic) to translate Celtic Spirituality into a usable form for today's seekers. Unlike beginners' guides now on the market, this book is an advanced study of the practice and expands on Conway's previous books about Celtic Spirituality.

$16.95 • Paper • ISBN 1-58091-073-4

Complete Guide to Tarot

By Cassandra Eason

Cassandra Eason makes a popular form of divination accessible and inviting, even for beginners and skeptics. She gradually builds to advanced topics, including cleansing a deck, keeping a tarot journal, analyzing complex spreads, and incorporating tarot into practices like the Kabbalah and numerology.

$18.95 • Paper • ISBN 1-58091-068-8

Crystal Enchantments: A Complete Guide to Stones and Their Magical Properties

By D. J. Conway

D. J. Conway's book will help guide you in your choice of stones from Adularia to Zircon, by listing their physical properties and magical uses. It will also appeal to folks who are not into magic, but simply love stones and want to know more about them.

$16.95 • Paper • ISBN 1-58091-010-6

Laying on of Stones

By D. J. Conway

Stones can be used to protect and heal you, your family, and your home, but where to place them is often a source of difficulty. Probably the most important question frequently asked is where to place them on your body. D. J. Conway has supplied you with forty detailed diagrams, showing you exactly how to place a variety of stones to help your body heal itself of illness or enrich your life through a magical manifestation of desires.

$10.95 • Paper • ISBN 1-58091-029-7

Spinning Spells, Weaving Wonders: Modern Magic for Everyday Life

By Patricia Telesco

This essential book of over 300 spells tells how to work with simple, easy-to-find components and focus creative energy to meet daily challenges with awareness, confidence, and humor.

$14.95 • Paper • ISBN 0-89594-803-6

The Wiccan Path: A Guide for the Solitary Practitioner

By Rae Beth

This is a guide to the ancient path of the village wise-woman. Writing in the form of letters to two apprentices, Rae Beth provides rituals for the key festivals of the wiccan calendar. She also describes the therapeutic powers of trancework and herbalism, and outlines the Pagan approach to finding a partner.

$12.95 • Paper • ISBN 0-89594-744-7

To receive a current catalog from The Crossing Press
please call toll-free, 800-777-1048.
Visit our Web site: **www.crossingpress.com**